Here's more about *It Takes a Home*

D0354578

"*It Takes a Home* provides important insights into creating a successful and productive home. It should be required reading for anyone who contemplates starting a family."

Thomas J. Stanley, Ph.D.
Author, *The Millionaire Mind, The Millionaire Next Door*

Nancy Parker Brummett is also the author of

Simply the Savior
The Journey of Elisa

If you have a comment, or would like to schedule Nancy to speak,
please contact her through Cook Communications,
or e-mail her at grancycomm@msn.com.

It Takes a

HOME

And Other Lessons
from the Heart

NANCY PARKER BRUMMETT

Cook Communications

Faithful Woman is an imprint of
Cook Communications Ministries, Colorado Springs, Colorado 80918
Cook Communications, Paris, Ontario
Kingsway Communications, Eastborne, England

IT TAKES A HOME

Printed in the United States of America.

Editor: Roberta Rand, Julie Smith
Cover Design: Boven Design Studio
Interior Design: Pat Miller

1 2 3 4 5 6 7 8 9 10 Printing/Year 04 03 02 01 00

LIbrary of Congress Cataloging-in-Publication Data

Brummett, Nancy Parker.
     It takes a home: and other lessons from the heart/by Nancy Parker Brummett.—1st U.S. ed.
     p. cm.
     ISBN 0-7814-3385-1
     1. Family—Religious aspects—Christianity. 2. Christian women—Religious life. I. Title.

     BT707.7 .B78 2000
     248.8'43—dc21   00—032993

Dedication

• • • • • • • • • • • • • • • •

Lovingly dedicated to my mother,
Lois Whitehead Parker,
whose face I always see
whenever I hear the word *home*.

Acknowledgments

· · · · · · · · · · · · · · · ·

What a gift it is to have friends and relatives willing to let me include snippets of their lives in this book. Thank you to each and every one.

I'm also grateful for my editor, Julie Smith, who consistently encouraged me to stretch further, reach higher, and dig deeper than I might have on my own. That's all you can ask of an editor or a friend, and I consider her both.

Several times in *It Takes a Home* I reference Barbara Mouser and her life-changing Bible study, *Five Aspects of Woman*. Reading the completed manuscript, however, I realize that the biblical truths Barbara's study revealed and explained to me are interwoven into every chapter. Her study opened my eyes to God's created purpose for women, home, and family as never before. Once I saw the truth I became passionate about sharing it with others. Since the result is this book, I am indebted to Barbara for her dedicated research into "the whole counsel of God," and the profound effect it has had on my life.

Other "truth seekers" who have influenced this work are the past and present pastors of Fellowship Bible Church in Colorado Springs, Colorado. I thank them for their faithfulness.

As always, my husband, Jim, played the role of encourager, prayer partner, computer expert, and critic during the writing process. No list of "thank yous" would be complete without his name. Thanks, Jim.

Contents

· · · · · · · · · · · · · · ·

Introduction

· · · · · · · · · · · · · · ·

W e need to celebrate and believe in homes again.
Just as there are no perfect people or perfect
families, there are no perfect homes. Our attempts
to create perfect homes will be met with cluttered cupboards and
dust bunnies at best, abuse and divorce at worst.

Yet to throw up our hands and abandon God's concept for a
life-giving home is to fail miserably. Rather we must accept that
the homes we build have a profound influence on our families,
and that the choices we make about our homes, and our roles in
them, have eternal significance.

Unfortunately, many of the messages the world delivers about
home and family are misguided and deceptive. When we listen to
them, we can easily lose sight of the true value of home. In the
'80s, I was a divorced, single mother of two boys. After a decade of
exposure to feminist philosophy, I bought into some of these

deceptive messages. Too often I thought of my home and parenting responsibilities as burdens, as interruptions to the life I wanted to live, rather than as God-given privileges.

Today, more women have come to understand that freedom of choice about family and career includes the freedom to choose to stay home. Some even understand that life has seasons, and that they can have it all, just not all at the same time. But there are other deceptive messages circulating too. The importance of home and family continues to be minimized in our culture, and parents are sometimes lulled into neglecting their primary responsibility, which is to ensure that their homes are healthy, productive, safe places for their children to live and grow.

"Home is the bottom line of life, the anvil upon which attitudes and convictions are hammered out—the single most influential force in our earthly existence. No price tag can adequately reflect its value," wrote Charles R. Swindoll in his book *Home: Where Life Makes Up Its Mind.*[1]

We know in our hearts that we can not abdicate this sacred responsibility for building a sound home and raising our children to any governmental agency or special interest group. Certainly, the "village" can provide us with resources and support, but it takes a home to raise happy, healthy children. It always has, and it always will.

Obviously, I didn't write *It Takes a Home* in order to brag about my perfect family or to tell you how to run yours. My purpose is not to make you feel guilty, convince you to quit your job, or discourage you from accepting your next promotion. Rather, I wrote it with a fervent prayer that sharing the truth the Lord has taught me through heartache and disappointment as well as through times of incredible joy and blessing will encourage you to make Christ-centered, heart-centered decisions about your home and your role in it.

I'll stop short of echoing the words of a caller to a radio talk show who admonished, "the only thing the village can raise is idiots!," but I certainly agree that our families are too precious to be turned over to the village. Creating a perfect home may not be possible, but abdicating our God-given responsibility to create the best homes we can is not an acceptable option.

We must continue to trust in the eternal value of one home under God, for it's only the home that can save our children from the destructive influences the village often promotes.

—Nancy Parker Brummett

A Home Defined

• • • • • • • • • • • • • •

Home interprets heaven;
Home is heaven for beginners.

—*Charles Henry Parkhurst*

What is home and how do we get there? Developers would have us believe it's a brand new house with a three-car garage. Those who live under a bridge might call a cardboard box home. But because a home is so much more than its physical structure, the word home holds connotations for each one of us that are defined by our hearts, not by the real estate sections in the local newspaper.

Whenever I hear the word home I think of the white, two-story frame house in Tennessee where I grew up. This is the house my parents brought me to as a newborn. It's the house where my sisters and I played dolls under the dining room table and where I talked to my friends on a black, rotary-dial telephone in the hallway.

This is the house where I chatted with my grandmother on the back porch while she snapped beans and dropped the pieces into a big aluminum bowl that seemed molded to her lap. We had our best talks on those lazy summer afternoons, and whenever I snap beans today, I'm immediately transported to a calm place in my heart and reconnected to her love and wisdom.

I consider the fact that I have such a home in my memory to be one of the greatest blessings of my life. My mother is in her eighties now and still lives in the same house, so it's possible for me to go home in a very real sense. I could still slide down the banister and climb the maple tree in the side yard if I wanted.

I've had many other homes, of course. As a young Army bride with babies, I created a home for my family in the temporary quarters in Germany—mail-order curtains, government-issued furniture and all. More apartments and five houses followed, including the one that sheltered my two boys and me during the seven years I was a single mom after my divorce.

The house I live and work in now is the brick rancher that my second (and last!) husband, Jim, and I moved into as soon as we could sell the homes we each owned. It was important for us to have a new place to begin life with our blended family. Since Jim had two teenage daughters and I had two teenage sons when we married, it was also important to find a house where the boys' bedrooms were as far away as possible from the girls' bedrooms! The walk-out lower level of this house provided the perfect male retreat, and put the boys on a separate floor entirely.

All four kids are married now, and six little trees are planted in the backyard in honor of the five precious granddaughters and one precious grandson who have joined our blended family. After serving as headquarters for graduations, weddings, Christmases, and Thanksgivings too numerous to count, this house has history—something very precious the second time around.

Sure there are cracks in the driveway, some of the windows don't shut quite right, and there's lots of redecorating I'd like to do someday, but I can see the sun rise over the prairie from one window and the moon setting behind the mountains from another. Since 1989, we've lived, loved, and grown through all the changes in our lives right here. This house is home.

When you close your eyes and think of home, I hope it doesn't take long for a kind memory to come back to you. Maybe it's the smell of Sunday pot roast, the rickrack on the edge of the curtains at the kitchen window, or a front porch step where you used to sit and wait for the school bus. Whatever your memories, cherish them.

It's heartbreaking to think that so many people don't have a single pleasant memory of a place they called home; a place where they could hang their hearts along with their hats.

I'm blessed and I know it. Maybe you are too. But those of you who haven't had the blessing of a home to love should take heart. It's not too late for you to create a home where you are now. And besides, our earthly homes are shanties compared to the home we will someday have in heaven.

Our Heavenly Home

For believers in Jesus Christ, home has an eternal definition. Since we are, as Paul wrote, only aliens here on earth, we don't have to be bound by earthly definitions of home.

"In my father's house are many rooms," Jesus told his disciples. "If it were not so, I would have told you. I am going there to prepare a place for you" (John 14:2). In other words, we already have a home so glorious it would astound the architects of the world's most opulent palaces.

Someone sent me a refrigerator magnet that reads: *Memo: Gone to Father's house to prepare your place—will be back soon to pick you up.—Jesus.* What a great reminder that we're only passing through, and heaven is our real home. He who had no home of His own on earth has gone to prepare our eternal one. And those who live in mansions now may be in rooms next to the homeless people they drive by every evening on the way home from work.

People with disabilities or in chronic pain here on earth seem more focused than most of us on their heavenly homes to come. "Suffering hurries the heart homeward,"[1] Joni Eareckson Tada, a quadriplegic since a diving accident in 1967, writes in her book *Heaven: Your Real Home.*

Reminding readers of all the glory to come, Joni says, "Let's not get too settled in, too satisfied with the good things down here on earth. They are only the tinkling sounds of the orchestra warming up. The real song is about to break into a heavenly symphony, and its prelude is only a few moments away."[2]

Until then, however, we will continue to establish and live in earthly homes. What makes a house a home, of course, are the people in it. And the kinds of homes that exist are as varied as the rooftops we see as we look down from an airplane flying over any city in America.

Homes with Heart

Some houses are home to more than one family and some, though they may be only temporary, are homes for the heart. I was privileged to be a part of the community group that established a Ronald McDonald House in Colorado Springs, Colorado. There are now over two hundred Ronald McDonald Houses in twenty countries providing a "home away from home" for families with sick children in nearby hospitals.

My long association with this organization taught me a lot about what makes a house a home. The Ronald McDonald House is known as The House That Love Built™. Indeed, it takes the love and dedication of an entire community to make a Ronald McDonald House a reality. Once the doors are opened, distraught families come inside to discover love, acceptance, comfort, and the protected, safe environment that truly defines home.

In the big kitchen of our House, it's common to see the grandmother of one sick child comforting and advising the young mother of a premature infant over a cup of tea. Related by circumstance only, these strangers soon form a nurturing, intergenerational bond so often missing in single family homes today.

After I left the board of the Ronald McDonald House, I decided the Lord was leading me to take what I had learned and help a struggling non-profit residential facility for single moms and their children. Family Life Services is a ministry housed in a stone and frame house built in 1905. Surrounding the main house are nine separate apartments.

Some of the moms and children who come to live at FLS for up to two years have suffered a lifetime of abuse and loss. Even the smallest children seem to carry scars of confusion and rejection. But the counseling and love they find at FLS is like salve to their wounds. Used furniture from an attic storeroom, some fresh paint brushed on the walls by church volunteers, and soon one of the tiny apartments is once again transformed into a home for a hurting family.

In the big yard outside, you can always hear the laughter of children playing. Nearby, their moms gather to share life stories and empathize with one another, creating a real sense of belonging. Again, it is the love, the acceptance, and the protected environment that make Family Life Services feel like home.

I'm sure there are similar houses in your community—or in your memory. Only people who have never entered the doors of such sanctuaries could think of them as less than real homes.

Cultural Changes in the Home

But what about the homes you and I live in? How do we make them homes with a heart instead of just so much brick and mortar? Our task is made difficult because we no longer live in a totally home-friendly culture. With both Dad and Mom often out of the house earning a living, and evening television distracting families from genuine communication, the potential demise of the American home is more than gloom and doom.

Sociological shifts occurring over the past half century provide us with insight into changes taking place in the American family and in our traditional definitions of home.

Attendees at the FamilyLife Marriage Conferences hosted by Campus Crusade for Christ from coast to coast are given a workbook for the three-day seminar. An outline in this workbook defines the changes in American culture from the 1950s to the 1990s, providing critical insight into what's happened to the home.[3] It explains how America has shifted from a rural culture to an urban one. Where the family was once the primary influence over children, it is now one of many competing influences. Likewise, our culture has moved from being God-centered and others-centered to being man-centered and self-centered. The traditional model for a family—once composed of a mom, a dad, and their biological children—has changed. In the 1990s, the traditional family model has come under attack and given way to a myriad of other models.

The roles of family members within the home have also changed dramatically. Marriage roles once clear and unchallenged have become confused. Fathers were traditionally serious providers and present in the '50s, but became passive providers often absent by the '90s. With the passing years, stay-at-home mothers, once valued and esteemed by society, have seen their roles demeaned and downplayed as women with careers became more visible and valued. Even the value placed on having children has shifted. Children were anticipated in the '50s, and childhood was protected. But by the '90s, children were considered optional, and childhood was hurried so parents could get on to other priorities.

In short, the traditional family of the '50s was imperfect but intact. Sociologists prone to pessimism see the family of today as imperfect and disintegrating.

Yet there is hope when we refuse to hand our families over to the "village" and hand them over to the Lord instead.

God's Plan for Homes

"Despite the blows it has taken over the decades, the home persists," writes Mary Farrar in her insightful book *Choices,* written for women seeking God's will for their lives. "It lives on as the heart of our nation. It stands ever-central, as the pivotal environment in which lives are shaped."[4]

Why is the home still standing when so many wolves are huffing and puffing in an attempt to blow it in? Because God wants it to stand. This isn't a new idea with Him. In Genesis 1:28, His concept for home was already in place when He made Adam and Eve co-partners in fulfilling His great mandate. We read, "God blessed them and said to them, 'Be fruitful and increase in number; fill the earth, and subdue it.' "

In Genesis 2:24, we see more of God's plan for marriage and family when He commands, "For this reason a man will leave his father and mother and be united to his wife, and they will become one flesh." From this union comes both the sanctity of marriage and our first glimpse at the home management team God put in place.

As discouraged as we may get about the future of the American home and family, we can find hope in knowing that God wants families to stay together, and He will do whatever it takes to keep the wolves away. God loves homes, and He loves the families who live in them. He will also give us the power we need to fight for our families when a battle is at hand.

"I believe we are now embroiled in the most pivotal battle of our generation, the fight for the soul of America," says Dennis Rainey, co-founder of FamilyLife. "This battle demands courage— the courage of husbands and wives who will turn from the seductive voices of the culture and make their marriages work; the backbone of dads and moms who will reject the poisons of materialism and shape the conscience and character of the next generation . . . There is hope! With God's help, we can get there from here."5

Yet even with God's support our families will never be perfect because they are made up of fallen people living in a fallen world. God knows that, which may be why He chose to show us some very nontraditional, even dysfunctional families in the Bible.

Worried about the way your two little boys roll around on the floor punching one another? Think about Cain and Abel's sibling rivalry! Wish your husband were as wise, poetic, and romantic as Solomon? How would you feel being one of thousands of wives?

There were other nontraditional families. The blended family Abraham oversaw included his wife Sarah, her son Isaac, her handmaid Hagar, and Hagar's son Ishmael. The family Jesus most loved spending time with was composed of two single sisters and their bachelor brother—Mary, Martha, and Lazarus. And we could even surmise that Aquila and Priscilla, a ministry couple known for their faithfulness to the early church, may have suffered the pain of childlessness. Yet God made the stories of all those families part of His eternal Word.

As believers, we know that our sanctification, our growth in Christ, will continue until we are with the Lord in His glory. Only then will we be perfect. The same is true of our families.

In the Christian home, we have the opportunity to establish what Charles Henry Parkhurst called "heaven for beginners." Our homes are not, and never will be, ideal. But just because we are incapable of achieving perfection we mustn't stop seeking God's purpose for the Christian home in the world today. He can use our imperfect families to spread His Word just as He used the less than perfect families in the Bible.

We must continue to allow God to use the families He has created to His glory—and He can use them all. To listen to the world's messages about marriage, raising children, and home life is to rob our society and our children of the only hope we have for living lives with eternal value.

What are these deceptive messages we hear that threaten our homes and families? The first is that marriage is a 50-50 proposition in which an individual spouse's "rights" are more important than a child's right to grow up in a family with both parents. The truth is that each person in a marriage has to give much more than 50 percent to make a relationship work. Anyone who's been happily married more than ten minutes can attest to that fact.

A second deceptive message is that strangers and institutions can raise our children as effectively as we can. The truth is, caring for children without caring about them sends all manner of sharp arrows into their delicate self-images.

It takes a home with parents who are committed to their marriage and their children first—far ahead of their professional goals and material desires—for children to feel valued.

Different Homes to Love

And it doesn't take a mansion to instill a feeling of home in any of us. If you've ever gone camping, you know the feeling you get after returning to the campsite after a long hike. From a distance, you see your familiar, old blue-and-white-checkered dishtowel waving in the breeze from the makeshift clothesline. You see the sagging green tent that you tossed and turned in the night before, and you know that, at least for now, you are home.

Even a church can be a home of sorts. Author Anne Lamott, in her book *Traveling Mercies,* tells about the church that became a home for her and her son as she made her way as a single mom.

"When I was at the end of my rope," she writes, "the people at St. Andrew tied a knot in it for me and helped me hold on. The church became my home in the old meaning of *home*—that it's where, when you show up, they have to let you in. They let me in.

They even said, 'You come back now.' "[6]

When a home falls apart, it takes a lot to put it together again. This is when the church can make a difference. So can secular institutions. I don't have a problem supporting those organizations in our communities, our "villages," that come alongside to help. I just balk at the idea that the primary responsibility for the health of a home and family belongs to third-party groups rather than to parents.

One of the most helpful of these organizations, CASA (Court Appointed Special Advocates), trains volunteers to assist children caught up in the pain of an abusive or disintegrating family. Interviewing all the adults involved and sitting with the child in courtroom hearings, the advocate offers to the court what he or she sees as the best solution for the long-term survival of the child, even if it means placement in a foster home.

As part of its tenth anniversary celebration, our local CASA chapter asked me to write a story that would help the children they work with sort through the feelings they have about the dramatic, often traumatic, changes in their lives. They wanted it to be a story that would reassure the children that there are many different kinds of homes and families, and that any home where they will be loved and safe is a good home.

I decided to write about a displaced prairie dog named Petey. Petey becomes separated from his own home and family when he's out on an adventure one day. A flash flood fills the ditch between him and his colony, making it impossible for him to go home. Soon Petey meets up with a friendly grandmother rabbit who accompanies him on his search for a new home.

Together, Gramma Bunsy, the rabbit, and Petey tour prairie dog burrows now inhabited by different types of prairie animals. The burrowing owls won't let Petey live with them because he can't turn his head all the way around like they can. The snakes are too scary for Petey to live with, as they often eat prairie dogs, and the burrow inhabited by a family of ferrets is much too crowded. Finally Gramma Bunsy and Petey find the perfect new home for him, one inhabited by a box turtle, a salamander, a spadefooted toad and, wonder of wonders, a young female prairie dog named Penny!

Petey says good-bye to his advocate, the grandmother rabbit, and settles in for a good night's sleep in his new home. It's a good home, because it's one where differences don't really matter, and everyone feels loved and safe.

Whether we are blessed to be in a traditional family or a blended family that looks more like Petey's, don't we all just want what Petey wanted? Don't we all just want a home where we feel accepted, loved, and safe?

What is home? More than anything, it's a family—a family composed of individuals supporting each other and living out God's purpose for their lives. No home will be perfect, but using Scripture to guide us, it is possible for us to build homes that honor the Lord and are fulfilling and lifegiving to all who hang their hearts therein.

Home Builders:

1. What are your clearest memories of the home you lived in as a very young child?
2. How do you define family? In what ways do you believe your own experiences shape your definition?
3. How do you envision your heavenly home?

2

A Home with a Mom

•••••••••••••••

Nothing can compare in beauty and wonder and
admirableness, and divinity itself, to the silent work
in obscure dwellings of faithful women bringing
their children to honor, virtue, and holiness.

—*Henry Ward Beecher*

W hat did Mother Teresa and Goldie Hawn have in
common? A great deal more than you probably
imagine.

When Mother Teresa received her Nobel Prize, she was asked,
"What can we do to promote world peace?" She replied, "Go home
and love your family."

Goldie Hawn once said, "Women are the healers and the
caretakers and the heart of a home. They are very powerful."

These two women, with their divergent lifestyles and spiritual
differences, shared a common understanding of the importance of
home and family to the future of society. They also understood how
important it is for children to grow up in a home with a mom.

When did so many of us lose sight of these facts? Why does
anyone need to tell us what we would have known all along if
we'd listened to our mothers . . . and to our hearts?

I think the confusion amongst those of us in the baby boomer generation began in the '70s and '80s when we women bought into the first great lie: You can have it all—marriage, motherhood, *and* career. By the beginning of the '90s, after over a decade of this exhausting "liberation," we were willing to admit that not only could we not have it all, we didn't even want all we had: stress, ulcers, and heart disease included.

After too many long days, late nights, fast-food meals, neglected kids, and disoriented husbands, women stopped believing they could have it all. Yet, not ready to give up completely on the dream, we decided to believe the message of the '90s: You can have some of all of it.

It's true. You can. But like lukewarm coffee, it's just not satisfying. Tired of feeling guilty at the office about what's not done at home and guilty at home about what's not done at work, moms gathered around the coffeepot either place today are more likely to be talking about flextime than about flexing their corporate muscles.

The wise woman who listens to her heart knows her life is one of seasons. Chances are she will live long enough to have it all—just not all at the same time. She knows that her first priority is her family. She recognizes that no one knows her children's needs or celebrates their joys like she does. She knows in her heart that the marriage partnership is the most important one there is. And she doesn't believe the lie that someone else can take care of her family just as well as she can.

Making Choices

The choices mothers must make about child care and working outside the home are agonizing ones. I've watched friends, co-workers, stepdaughters, and daughters-in-law struggle with the same issues I faced as a mom with young children, and the struggles never seem to get any easier. If we marry and have children, will we continue to work outside the home? And if we work, will it be full time, part time, or from a home office? Before feeling too sorry for ourselves, however, it's important to remember that just having such choices is an incredible privilege.

Certainly, many women have to work at jobs they don't particularly enjoy just to keep a roof over the family's head and food on the table. A single mom who is the sole support of her family usually has fewer economic options than the married mom does. Many moms have no choice at all, and so this debate is not directed at them.

But the mothers who would only have to sacrifice some of their wants, not their needs, to spend more time at home *do* have a choice. And they need to make it with their eyes wide open, keenly aware of the irreplaceable role moms play. For when it's all sorted out, the importance of the mother in the home cannot be denied. In the hearts of our children, plain and simple, home is a place with a mom in it. It always has been and it always will be.

The greatest injustice our society can do to a woman is not the unequal paycheck or gender bias in the workplace. It's the message that being a mother is not in itself a full-time, worthwhile job, and being available to your children is not as important as spending your waking hours at a desk or on an assembly line. How very wrong that is.

Of course, it's equally wrong to hold to the position that every mother of children must be at home full time. Each woman must make her own choices, in consultation with her God and her husband, if she has one, and then be prepared to live with the outcome. But the decision should be carefully weighed and prayed about, and not based simply on a "grass is greener" impulse.

What I've observed is that women whose closets are full of corporate suits and sensible pumps often yearn for the comfort of a "soccer mom" ensemble. Yet, the soccer mom, picking up snacks for the game at the grocery store, looks at these attractively dressed working women with envy. "That looks like more fun," she thinks. Certainly the decision of whether to work outside the home deserves much more thought.

Some women arrive at their decision easily. They are so certain they would be miserable in the home that they are almost afraid to give it a try. "I'm a more patient, caring mother because I work outside the home," they say. Maybe this is true—or maybe it's a rationalization for choosing an easier life than being a full-time mom. Their consolation is the illusory concept of "quality time." But what is quality time, really? And can we ever schedule it?

"As I've said for years," writes Brenda Hunter in her book *The Power of Mother Love,* "quality time grows out of the soil of quantity time. We need to be with our babies, toddlers, preteens and adolescents for hours or even days before we experience those fleeting golden moments known as quality time."[1]

The truth is, there is no substitute for a mother in a child's life. This is true of children of all ages. Babies don't really know whether a mother is present or not, the argument goes, so they are fine in day care. But psychologist Lee Salk says the reverse is true. Babies really don't understand the concept of time. They can't understand that if you go away you will come back. "If he cannot see you, you are no longer there; in fact, you don't exist," Salk says.[2]

The elementary school-aged child may gain independent living skills in child care or latchkey situations, but at what cost? Will the same child also be withdrawn, and so independent that she surrounds herself with a protective wall few can scale?

Those who think teenagers don't need close supervision simply haven't had teenagers. Never is being available more critical than during the teenage years. How are your teens spending their discretionary time? With whom? These are critical questions that can't be answered over the phone from work.

By the time a woman is ready to make a choice about if and how much she will work outside the home, she has already made several significant decisions that impact her life and the lives of those she loves. These decisions not only shape who she is; they have the power to significantly influence her marriage, her family, and her home.

In the nineteenth century, the philosopher Henri-Frederic Amiel wrote, "Woman is the salvation or the destruction of the family. She carries its destiny in the folds of her mantle." We no longer wear mantles, but the statement is still true. Are we contributing to our family's salvation or its destruction?

A Woman's Decisions

Most women sooner or later face the decision of whether to get married. If they marry, then comes the important decision of whether to become a mother. Granted, some give the decision more forethought than others, but when the answer is yes, and a baby is placed in a woman's arms in the hospital delivery room or the adoption agency office, she will never be the same again.

A wonderful story about motherhood is attributed to "anonymous," which is fitting because any mother could have written it. Two women are having lunch. One is already a mom, the other is not. "I'm taking a survey," the childless woman says half jokingly. "Do you think I should have a baby?"

Before responding, the mom flashes on all the scenarios of motherhood that she has experienced, and that she knows her friend will too. She looks across the table at her friend's carefully manicured nails and stylish suit.

"I want to tell her that the physical wounds of childbearing heal, but that becoming a mother will leave her with an emotional wound so raw that she will be forever vulnerable," the mother writes.

"I want to describe to my friend the exhilaration of seeing your child learn to ride a bike. I want to capture for her the belly laugh of a baby who is touching the soft fur of a dog or cat for the first time. I want her to taste the joy that is so real, it actually hurts."

When her friend's quizzical look makes the mom realize tears have formed in her eyes, she reaches across the table, squeezes her friend's hand, and simply says, "You'll never regret it." Then she offers a silent prayer for her friend, and for herself, and for "all the mere mortal women who stumble their way into this most wonderful of callings. The blessed gift of being a mother."

Could it be that the problem we have with child care in this country stems from the fact that too many women today are entering into motherhood without giving it the priority that it deserves? They put it on a list of life's goals, giving it no greater credence than receiving a promotion at work, buying a new car, or touring Europe. Or they see becoming a mother as the fulfillment of a dream—like winning the lottery. They consider the time they take off to be with a newborn to be nothing more than a bump on their carefully chosen career paths or life journeys. But unless they get enough anesthesia during delivery to numb their hearts along with their episiotomy incisions, they are in for a big surprise.

Just ask the mom of a six week old who has just dropped him off at day care so she can go back to work for the first time since he was born. If she makes it to the office without calling to check on him, she's showing great restraint—or she can't see to dial her cell phone through her tears.

In the best of worlds, when mom isn't home to take care of the kids, grandma is. But we all know that today's grandmas (myself included) aren't always geographically available to help out, or they have agendas of their own that don't include full-time baby-sitting.

So eventually, for the career-oriented woman with the privilege of choice, saying yes to motherhood means deciding about child care. Just as any decision is made more effectively when we take the time to analytically list the pros and cons, the decision about working and placing your children in child care versus caring for them yourself can be made in much the same way. The only difference is that the items listed on each side of the yellow legal pad come not just from the mind, but from the heart.

If you find yourself at this crossroads, here's how it works. On one side list everything you will have to give up if you quit your job to stay at home with your children. Income will be on the list. So might a newer car, a larger house, or more expensive vacations. Don't forget self-esteem, ego-boosting career advancements, and daily interaction with stimulating adults.

Now list what your child will have to give up if you are not a part of her daily life. Think back to your own childhood for clues. If your mom was at home with you, what do you remember most fondly about that time? If she wasn't, what do you remember missing? A hug after school? Lazy summer mornings? Showing off an A on a school paper? Which list has more real value?

Whatever you decide, don't buy into the lie that quality child care is just as effective as parenting. Experts have always agreed that the critically formative years for children are from birth to age three—exactly when most working moms are entrusting their little ones to day care. When a study was released proclaiming that mothers who work outside of the home during the first three years of their children's lives do not harm their youngsters' development, columnist Kathleen Parker's studied response was, "Phooey."

First, she exposed the fallacies in the research itself, pointing out that half of the sample were single mothers. A significant percentage of the children were also from lower-income families, and additionally, they had mothers of less than average intelligence.

"Most mothers understand instinctively what's best for their children, and most do the best they can," Parker summarized. "If a mother has to work and needs day care to provide for her children, no one can blame her wishing for reassurance that her child won't be damaged. In most cases, common sense tells us that well-loved children well cared for will not necessarily maim small animals," she wrote.

"But common sense also tells us that a mother's intransigent love cannot be approximated by even the most attentive hired help," Parker continued. "No study will ever otherwise convince me or millions of other mothers who know better."[3]

Again, when making the decision about child care, listen to your heart. Consider not only what your child may miss by being out of your presence during the day, but what you will miss as well.

How many two-month-old babies have flashed their precious first smiles at child care workers too busy to notice? How many one year olds have risked first steps in the direction of a child care provider who doesn't even know a milestone has been reached? Where's the joy, the celebration, and the snapshot sessions this little soul so richly deserves? And where's the mother who should be holding out her arms and smiling through tears of pride and joy?

Even mothers of older children can miss so much.

The day before I left my job after sixteen years, I had to face up to the one task I dreaded most: cleaning out my desk drawer. The contents were melded into one giant rectangle of paper clips, rubber bands, plastic spoons, push pins, and cough drops.

Within this moraine of corporate life, however, I discovered a treasure: a three-inch button with a picture of my son Tim in his Little League baseball uniform. In the photo, he's wearing a hat three sizes too big and a sideways smile on his nine-year-old face that seems to say, "I don't know if I can hit *or* catch a ball, but I'm sure going to try."

All moms know the memories that button evokes. Most of them are positive for me, because I loved being a part of it all . . . the ball games, pack meetings, band concerts. However, the challenges of being a single mom were great. The schedules were always posted on the refrigerator, but the times seemed impossible to meet.

But along with the memories comes the guilt. Why was I

always so late getting to the games? It was possible for me to leave work on time, but too often I didn't. I actually remember frantically slicing oranges for the team treat on the passenger seat of my car as I drove down the interstate.

Fortunately, our kids tend to grow up to appreciate our best efforts and forgive us for being less than perfect. One Mother's Day while Tim was away at college, I received a card from him that I treasure even more than the button. On the cover is a photo of two little boys in baseball gear. Inside the blank card he wrote: "Just like me, huh? Happy Mom's Day, Mom! Thanks for bringin' the oranges! Love always, Tim." The forgiveness is wonderful, but my prayer for those of you who still have choices to make is that you won't lose sight of what matters most in the first place.

Gratefully, more and more moms with outside jobs are entering their kids' special activities into their daily planners–and leaving work to attend them! If you're one of these privileged parents, resolve to leave work on time. Be a first-inning mom. Be in your seat when the curtain rises. In ten years, you won't be able to remember what was important enough to keep you at work. I guarantee it.

Reviewing the Decision

If you are a mom working outside the home, I encourage you to reconsider your decision to be away from your children more often than I did. If finances allow, or you can learn to live with fewer material luxuries, it's a decision that's reversible. It needs to be reviewed from time to time as your family changes.

In an essay titled "Romancing the Mom," Christine Dubois writes about going back to visit the office she left when she decided to stay home with her newborn son. At first when she enters her old office she admits to being "caught up in the romance of it all." But then she realizes how little has changed, and how little she has really missed.

"I remember cleaning out my files after I resigned, tossing stacks of urgent, confidential, and top priority correspondence into the recycling bin," she wrote. "One weighty file was devoted to the Communications Strategic Planning Task Force. Six months of meetings, memos, and resolutions. Then the vice president who chaired the task force was laid off, and the whole project died. I had nothing to show for it but a file I couldn't quite bear to throw out.

"On the other hand, six months of rocking, nursing, and changing diapers produces lasting and noticeable results. In six months, an infant sits up. Another six months, and he's beginning to walk. Six months more, and he's starting to talk. Suddenly, he's not a baby anymore."

Ms. Dubois concludes her essay by saying, "The choices women face today are complex. But we can't afford to let society define success for us. We must shake off our infatuation with the business world and learn to listen to our hearts. After two years away, I still feel the lure of the FAX machines and business suits. But I can honestly say I'd rather talk to Lucas [her son] than meet with VIPs, rather read *Humpty Dumpty* than study a top-secret memo, rather eat peanut butter and jelly than dine in the company cafeteria."[4]

The decision of whether to work outside the home will always be easier for those of us who can keep the perspective that nothing is forever, and that the decisions we make can always be reconsidered.

Two stories that were in the national news at the same time seemed to say everything there is to say about the on-again, off-again journey of being a career woman today. The first was about a little girl who got on a train; the second about a grown woman who decided it was time to get off one.

The little girl was four years old and lived in Denver. Unbeknownst to her baby-sitter, she bravely decided to wander to the station, wearing only a T-shirt, socks, and underwear, and climb aboard the light rail train she often rode with her mother—only this time, she was all alone.

After being rescued by authorities and spending the night in a crisis center, she was reunited with her mother. Watching this story, our collective response was one of relief and amusement: relief that the toddler was safe, amusement that she had the presence of mind and self-confidence to climb aboard a train all by herself. To raise little girls with such a sense of adventure is positive and wonderful, and it's something today's parents seem to be doing extremely well. I see this amazing spirit in my own little granddaughters as they approach every new experience with an "I can do it" attitude. It gets them on the train.

But the second story is of Brenda Barnes, forty-three-year-old president and chief executive officer of PepsiCo. In September 1997, she announced she was leaving her prestigious position as one of the highest-ranking women in corporate America to go home and spend more time with her husband and three children, ages seven, eight, and ten.

"Her departure from the fast track is sure to spark debate about how executives, especially dual-career couples, juggle work and family," stated the story of her announcement in the *Wall Street Journal,* but Ms. Barnes saw no reason for such debate.

"I hope people can look at my decision not as 'women can't do it' but 'for twenty-two years Brenda gave it her all and did a lot of great things,'" she said when questioned by reporters. Recounting her years of hectic travel, missed children's birthdays, and even living in separate cities from her husband as they both pursued high-powered careers, Ms. Barnes spoke of all the trade-offs she had made for PepsiCo.

"Now I need to give my family more of my time," she stated matter-of-factly, adding that it wasn't so much that her children needed her, but that she needed them.[5]

What I saw in these news stories were two women on oppo-site ends of the same journey, making as much out of life in the moment as they possibly could.

One was a woman-in-training with the confidence to climb on a train she thought would take her some place exciting. Not concerned about being dressed for success, she simply knew she wanted to ride the train—to find out where it would take her, and what she could see along the way.

The other was an amazingly successful woman with the judg-ment and sense to know when to get off the train. She had spent half her years on the fast track. Finally realizing that too much of life was passing her by in a blur, she simply pulled the cord.

A mom I know gave up a job she loved because summer was coming and she couldn't bear to think of her boys cooped up in day care instead of playing outside. She knew it would mean tighter economic times for her family, but she also knew the benefits would be many.

I can't wish more for all the educated, talented young women I know than that they would have both the courage to get on the train when they want to, and the wisdom to know when it's time to get off.

A Time for Everything

"To everything there is a season," says Ecclesiastes 3:1 (KJV). For women, this often translates to a time to pursue a career, and a time to go home. After all, nothing is forever. "If I get the forty additional years statisticians say are likely coming to me," writes author Anna Quindlen, "I could fit in at least one, maybe two new lifetimes. Sad that only one of those lifetimes can include being the mother of young children."[6]

Mothers of small children grow weary of hearing, "Enjoy them. They grow up so fast," but it's just one of those inevitable facts of life older women feel compelled to pass along. I don't say it to admonish younger moms to be more appreciative of what they have. I say it because it's true, and I don't want them to make the mistake of wishing away the toddler years or the elementary school years. I want them to do a better job than I did of being present in the moment.

The song "Sunrise, Sunset" always makes me cry, especially when it's sung at weddings. "Where is the little girl I carried? Where is the little boy at play? I don't remember growing older. When did they?"

In the movie *Father of the Bride* (which came out some time during the five years in which we had four family weddings), Steve Martin is looking across the dinner table at his daughter as she announces to the family that she's getting married. As he looks at her, he sees not a sophisticated young woman dressed to go out with her intended, but a little girl with pigtails and freckles.

It's absolutely mind-boggling, not to mention heart rending, that the time goes by so quickly. It seems as if you're reading *Go, Dog, Go* and other Dr. Seuss favorites one minute, and college catalogs the next.

There have been times when one of my grown sons has greeted me with news like, "I asked her to marry me and she said yes!" or, "I got the job!" and my heart hears the same little voice that rushed into the kitchen to announce, "Mom, come look! There's a rainbow in the sky!"

Maybe knowing that the time goes by so quickly will encourage mothers to delay entering or re-entering the workforce until their children are older. If so, I also pray that a clear understanding of and belief in their significance in God's eyes will keep those same moms from doubting their worth during those stay-at-home years.

When my boys were little, we would recite the nursery rhyme, "To market, to market, to buy a fat pig. Home again, home again, jiggity jig." Many women today are discovering that the fat pig isn't as desirable as they thought, and the sacrifices required to bring home some bacon are far too great. They are joyfully coming "home again, home again, jiggity jig."

Going home represents a sacrifice too, but the sacrifice that accomplishes the desires of your heart hardly feels like a sacrifice at all.

A bittersweet story speaks of one mother's sacrificial love. After the monumental forest fire in Yellowstone National Park several years ago, forest rangers began their trek up a mountain to assess the inferno's damage. One ranger found a bird literally petrified in the ashes, perched statuesquely on the ground at the base of a tree. Unsettled by the eerie sight, he knocked over the bird with a stick. When he struck it, three tiny chicks scurried from under their dead mother's wings. The mother could have flown to safety, but she had refused to abandon her babies. When we are fortunate enough to have a choice and make the hard decision to stay at home rather than retreat to the relative quiet, safety, and sanctity of the carpeted office cubicle, we are making a sacrifice for our children too. One that may be equally lifegiving.

"No one can ever replace you in your children's lives," Brenda Hunter reminds us. "For them, you are the sun, the moon, the whole universe. You are your children's only mother, and if you are too often absent, harried, or preoccupied, they may yearn for you all of their lives."[7]

The decision to work outside the home may be a sound one. It's not my intent to make you feel guilty if you are such a working mother. But I do want to encourage you to be more aware than I was of the awesome, God-given purpose and power you have as the mom in your home.

Keep an "at home" attitude in the midst of the most challenging of careers or the most mundane of jobs. Don't give the best of your time and talents to strangers, leaving little energy for the husband and children longing for your presence in their lives. Look for ways to spend as much time at home as possible. Be emotionally available when you are present. Make yours a home with a mom.

A young mother in our neighborhood makes it a daily habit to walk her school-age daughter to the bus stop every morning. In the afternoon, she walks down to meet the bus, and together the two of them walk up the hill to their home. Usually the mom has her head tilted down listening as the little girl excitedly talks about her day, her backpack bouncing along behind her. One day, however, I watched as the two of them held hands and skipped all the way up the hill.

Regretably, the choices I made kept me from being that kind of a mom all the time. That I can now be that kind of grandmother is a gift I don't take for granted. Think about it. Would cutting back on your hours make it possible for you to meet a few school buses?

Economic realities exist. Life is full of hard choices. But before we make them, we need to pray about them. We need to listen to wise women like Mother Teresa and Goldie Hawn . . . and we need to listen to our hearts. If we listen closely enough, we just might hear the sound of a child skipping.

Home Builders:

1. What's the first thing that comes to mind when you think of your mother?
2. If you are a mom with children at home now, what messages do you hear in your heart regarding your importance to your children?
3. What if any changes do you want to make in order to make the most of your "mom years"?

A Home with a Dad

• • • • • • • • • • • • • •

A child is not likely to find a father in God unless
he finds something of God in his father.

—*Austin L. Sorenson*

My husband was installing one of those lighted ceiling fans above our kitchen table. The parts and instructions were scattered all over the table and the floor. The instructions called for him to connect a grounding wire to the wire coming out of the ceiling. This seemed pretty important to us, so we were trying to make sure it was done right. But the space was small and it was hard for Jim to see what he was doing.

"Could you hold the flashlight so I can see better?" he asked.

That's a simple task, one I was glad to perform since the ceiling fan was my bright idea in the first place. But as soon as I started holding that flashlight, working hard to get the beam exactly where it needed to be, I was no longer a fifty-one-year-old mother and grandmother holding a flashlight for her husband of eleven years. I was an eight-year-old girl holding the flashlight for my dad while he did one of his many chores around the house. Hold it just right, and

I could win his approval. Let the beam drift to the right or the left, and I might have to hear, once again, how he wished he had sons to help with his chores.

How profoundly the memories we have of our dads impact who we are. How critically they define and influence the image we have of our Heavenly Father.

My father excelled in being the authority figure in our house, so I never have a problem grasping the sovereign authority of God. But like many men of his generation, he wasn't quite as accomplished at expressing compassion and love, or at dispensing mercy and grace. I never doubted that my father loved me, but he never told me so except in writing.

Every Saturday morning my two sisters and I would sit around the breakfast table knowing what was coming. Before the meal was over, my dad would inevitably say, "Since I don't have any sons to help with the chores, which one of you girls is going to help me today?" Whoever didn't have a good excuse got stuck mowing the lawn or, in my case, holding the flashlight.

My sisters and I probably still do not fully realize what our father's seeming disappointment in our gender did to our self-concepts. I just know I only recently came to understand how completely God values women. Seeing how Jesus spoke to women and how He cherished them is what finally led me to grasp my worth in God's eyes. It's by receiving His grace and mercy that I know I am of equal importance to men. Designed for different purposes and roles in God's ordained order, yes, but equally valued, equally important, and equally loved.

In spite of his shortcomings (and all earthly fathers have them), my father was a consistent, stable presence in our home. He believed in right and wrong, was a loyal patriot, and served both the Lord and his family.

Apart from his authoritative manner that sometimes sent us scurrying to our rooms, I remember many positive things about my father. I loved to watch his capable hands at work. Samples I have of his strong, fluid handwriting are among my most treasured possessions—especially the letters that say, "I love you," or more frequently, "Your mother and I love you." I remember the way his eyes crinkled on the sides when he laughed and how his laugh could fill up a whole room. How welcome my dad's laughter was to my ears.

As he grew older, more comfortable with life's disappointments, and more honest about his own shortcomings, my dad mellowed. He also reached out more. He was my staunchest defender during my divorce, far more fervent in his defense than I deserved.

Standing behind a man at the post office shortly after my dad died, I realized how similar the man's build was to my tall, handsome father's. He was also about the age my dad had been when he died of heart failure. I wanted to tap the man on the shoulder and ask him to give me a hug, but instead I just stood quietly in line and let my eyes fill up with tears.

My father's been gone fourteen years and I still miss him dearly. I had a dedicated dad, and for that I am very grateful.

Do I believe it is possible for children to grow up successfully in a home without a dad present? Yes, I do. Certainly there are many single mothers proving that day after difficult day. But remember, *It Takes a Home* is a book about God's intended plan for us. Catch any single mother at a time when she's emotionally secure enough to be honest about her situation and she will confess what her heart knows: this isn't the way it was supposed to be.

A House Divided

Some images in life are permanently etched in our memories and in our hearts. One of mine is of my first husband pulling out onto the street where we lived, his '77 Scout packed to the hilt with extra dishes, pots and pans, and towels. One of our family's two golden retrievers looked mournfully out the back window. He, too, was a part of the division of property.

I stood in the street unable to move to go back in the house where I knew our boys, then almost eight and eleven, were waiting for me. But I did, and then somehow I managed to get the three of us to my older son's soccer game that afternoon. Sitting on the grass with the other parents with a lump in my throat as big as the ball on the field, the reality of the situation hit me. The children I had tried to protect from germs, evil strangers, and speeding automobiles had just been dealt one of the hardest blows life could deliver. And their own parents had done it to them.

Ours was declared a no-fault divorce, but as most are, it was really double-fault. The details don't matter. We married young and we were ignorant about the impact Satan can have on a marriage. We didn't know he roamed the earth delighting in destroying families. We both attended church, yes, but we hadn't asked Jesus Christ to be Lord of our lives all week long. The void that oversight left was quickly filled by Satan, who quite simply made our marriage his playground.

Now I had to face the harsh realization that I was the mother of "fatherless" children. Sure, their father provided for them financially and stayed as involved as any father can who lives across the country. They visited him during summers and holidays, but when it came to the day-to-day presence of a father in our home, they were, for all practical purposes, "fatherless."

Differences Between Moms and Dads

Any single mother, especially of boys, can tell you the problems that arise when moms have to be dads too. First of all, moms and dads are different so they are good at different things. I heartily disagree with gender-neutral advocates who say that boys and girls are basically the same. I've seen too many tiny girls cradle dolls and too many little boys pick up sticks and shout "bang-bang" to believe that it's our culture that creates gender differences. God creates women to excel at being feminine and men to excel at being masculine, and He planned for every home to have both a man and a woman in residence.

Women tend to want men to be one of two things: like God, or like women. Obviously, they can't be either, so women who hold to these expectations are guaranteed disappointment.

Yet a woman and a man each make unique contributions to the home that the other can only attempt to duplicate. And nothing spotlights the value of these unique gifts more quickly than single parenthood.

As a single mother I was good at keeping up with birthdays and holiday traditions, earning an income, planning the vacations, etc. But no matter how hard I tried to fill the void, I was a mom. And there were just times when a dad was needed.

Like the time we showed up at my son's first Cub Scout Pinewood Derby. In case you haven't had this experience, the Pinewood Derby is a race. Each scout is to make a race car from a kit containing a block of wood, four wheels, and a couple of axles. I was extremely proud of the fact that we managed to get the wheels hammered onto the block of wood and that all four of them moved forward together. That was until I saw all the other sleekly sanded and shaped, hand-painted sports cars. Clearly, dads had been involved in crafting them.

Whether it was kinetic energy or God's direct intervention, my son's car wasn't dead last—but it was close. The next year, a kind neighbor across the street took on the project and saved us the embarrassment of showing up with another block of wood with wheels.

Single moms soon learn the value of involving such neighbors, brothers, and granddads in their children's daily lives. Organizations like Big Brothers also help fill the void when the extended family can't. The need is there because moms aren't always good at dad things—and dads aren't always good at mom things.

Those who know my second husband and me are always amazed at how parallel our lives were before we met. Both of our first marriages lasted thirteen years. He had two girls three years apart, I had two boys three years apart. When we married seven years after my divorce and eight years after his, after dating for over three years, our blended family of four teenagers was like *The Brady Bunch.*

So about the time I was struggling with Pinewood Derby cars and trying to compensate for father-son campouts, Jim was across town deciding how to celebrate his oldest daughter's coming of age as a woman. He had joint custody of his girls, so they spent two weeks with his ex-wife and two weeks with him. Wouldn't you know, daughter number one started her first period while she was at dad's house. My husband, wanting so much to do the right thing and honor his daughter's advent to womanhood, baked her a cake and planned a "period party" for her.

Now I believe in being open and celebratory about coming-of-age milestones, but any woman would cringe picturing herself at a "period party" planned by her dad. Because she went through it herself, a mom knows how embarrassing all aspects of menstruation are to adolescent girls, and how important privacy is to them. A mom might have planned a special shopping trip with her daughter, followed by tea at a ritzy restaurant. Perhaps she would have shared some of her own experiences about being a woman. But a "period party"? God love him for trying.

I have great respect for all the men today who are determined to be involved, sensitive, loving dads to their children—and for the women who let them do it. That is what God intended when He gave to both Adam and Eve the great mandate to go forth and multiply. He had a plan, and like all the other plans God put into place, living out *His* plan is far more fruitful and fulfilling—and far less painful—than creating our own.

When a man becomes a dad, his wife will have many new reasons to fall in love with him all over again. Simple things like standing at the kitchen window watching her husband playing with the children in the backyard can make her eyes fill up with tears.

One of my favorite photographs from our first visit with our sixth grandchild, Charlie, is of his father joining his newborn son on the floor under his miniature toy gym. The plastic figures hanging from the gym were dangling on Scott's head, but he didn't care. He just gazed at his little son. Whenever they were alone together, I would overhear Scott pretending to give three-week-old Charlie lessons about "guy stuff."

"Okay, in football, you have four tries to make a first down," he would say. Or, "Remember, when you're fly-fishing, you have to keep your line taut."

My stepdaughter Joelle was keeping Charlie well fed and dry and wrapping him in the warmth of mother love. But her husband, while taking his turn at changing diapers, was clueing Charlie in on the things he thought he should know. And no one is better qualified to do that than the dad who loves him. "One father is more than a hundred schoolmasters," wrote George Herbert. The wise mom knows that's true, and she supports her husband's attempts to teach his children.

It's wonderful to see young dads like the ones in our family taking an active part in all aspects of child rearing. They are far more nurturing and loving than the sometimes emotionally or physically distant dads of my father's generation.

In his book *The Kid-Friendly Dad,* Frank Martin, himself a loving dad, writes that the kid-friendly dad "knows how to be much more than a father. He can be a shepherd, consultant, adviser, counselor, teacher, model, anchor, beacon and friend."[1] But even the new, modern, do-it-all dads are better at being dads than at being moms.

Our two oldest granddaughters have long, straight hair, and their mother is wonderfully adept at keeping it combed, creatively braided, or pulled back with cute clips and clasps.

One day the girls burst into our house after a two-day camping trip with their dad (my son Rob). I almost gasped at their appearance. Their hair obviously hadn't been brushed in two days, and the tangles were visible from across the room. Their jeans and T-shirts were caked with mud, as were their tennis shoes. With dirty faces and grimy hands they ran to give me hugs. Then I noticed the glow in their eyes and the rosy cheeks underneath the dirt. They had just had a wonderful adventure with their dad, and the tangles and dirt didn't matter at all.

Rob, who is great about helping with bath time, stories, and meals for the girls at home, had obviously declared the two-day trip a break from the usual routine.

"I guess they're kind of dirty," he offered apologetically. "They've been in the same clothes for two days." After a bath and a load of laundry, all the visible signs of the two-day, outdoor adventure were gone. But Francesca and Amanda were still showing me the rocks they had found. Over and over they told me about the snake they saw—and how their dad taught them to back up slowly. The girls won't really appreciate the time their dad is giving them until they have children of their own. Then their memories of days spent with him will be a heritage too precious to measure.

Making Room for Marriage

I was probably drawn to the book *The Lady, Her Lover, and Her Lord* by T.D. Jakes by its catchy title. But when I opened it, I began reading with skepticism. What could this male preacher possibly teach me about being a better wife? The answer? Everything.

Remember having a friend who was a boy when you were in school? Not a boyfriend, but a friend who was a boy. The one boy who would tell you how all boys really felt about girls and about life. This is what we women have in Bishop Jakes.

While he mourns the loss of true ladies in our society, he

understands why so many of us have abandoned our created purpose in order to compete with, and be more like men.

"The enemy has tried for years to wage a war between the sexes. He has tried in our boardrooms, our bedrooms, and even our pulpits. We must realize we were designed to work together. Our strength is in the variance of our strategies," Jakes writes.[2]

Yet for all his support of created gender roles, Jakes encourages women to be all God intended them to be in the Proverbs 31 sense of the excellent woman. He advises women to marry men with hands strong enough to clap for their successes.

"My advice to a man who is married to an ambitious woman is simple: applaud her strength and fill her voids. She has them. We all do. To the woman I say, make sure that the room [that is vacant] in your life is well lit and easy for him to see. Do not spend your life trying to prove to someone whom you love that you do not need him, because he just may believe you and walk away."[3]

And when he walks away, the result is the single-parent home with "fatherless" children. The woman left behind not only loses the constant presence of the father of her children, she loses her marriage.

Every year, thousands of women in this country find themselves adding "single mother" to their list of identifying labels—not by choice, but as a result of circumstances outside their control or the consequences of their own sin or that of their husbands. When these women put their hearts and souls into holding what's left of their families together, there is no more honorable job in our society than the one they perform.

Christians and Jews are called to "defend the cause of the fatherless" (Isa.1:17). Many churches and synagogues have outstanding programs for providing single mothers with the financial and emotional support they need. But I have a hard time feeling the same admiration for, and obligation to help, the women who become single mothers by choice.

Just when we thought Hollywood had thrown our society every negative influence available, they invented a new one: the celebrity single mom. I can understand a woman's desire to be a mother. I can even understand and applaud a woman not putting her life on hold just because the right man hasn't come along. She should buy the negligee and the good dishes. She should buy a home of her own if she can afford to do so. But the decision to have a child alone in order to check that off the list of life experiences she wants to have seems far more selfish than accomplished.

Columnist Kathleen Parker put into words what many of us were thinking when Jody Foster announced that she was going to have a baby and planned to raise it alone.

"Today, having a baby is like swinging through McDonald's for a burger," Parker writes. "One baby all the way, hold the dad." Parker goes on to say that the fact that Foster will be a good mom, as her friends report, is beside the point.

"What's appalling is our mindless celebration of single motherhood at a time when fatherlessness is a national crisis," she writes. "On any given day in any American city, a fatherless boy is booked on murder charges. A barely pubescent girl gives birth to another fatherless infant. Like morons unable to connect the numbered dots, we continue to treat each celebrity announcement of single motherhood as a virgin event. You can practically hear the cattle lowing in yonder manger."[4]

Dads Matter

It isn't just the stars like Foster, Madonna, and Diane Keaton who have promoted the idea that fathers are dispensable. The producers of Hollywood's TV programs have as well.

According to a study conducted by the National Fatherhood Initiative in 1999, our children and grandchildren were far more likely to encounter a homosexual male character on prime-time TV than a competent father. Out of more than one hundred prime-time network shows, fifteen featured fathers as recurring, central characters—with only four of those fathers considered to be positive role models by the group. In comparison, there were twenty-five homosexual, bisexual, or transgendered characters on the networks' prime-time shows.[5]

"The absence of good TV dads is a concern because a substantial number of young men are now growing up clueless about what their primary role in the future family will be: that of a father. At a time when children badly need fathers . . . the networks portray them as missing, confused, aloof or completely uninformed," said the group's chairman, Don Eberley, in a report to *USA Today*.[6]

The wise mother and wife knows how important it is to have a strong dad in the home. It matters to her, and it matters to her children. Equally important, it matters to him.

"That man is a success who has lived well, laughed often, and loved much; who has gained the respect of intelligent men and the love of children," Robert Louis Stevenson wrote. A man who truly wants to enjoy the kind of success that adds value to his life and brings glory to his God knows he has to begin at home. Fortunately, there are organizations dedicated to giving him the support he needs and deserves.

The problem of the missing father has birthed several groups dedicated to bringing these fathers back into the picture and to helping men still in the home feel better equipped to accept their responsibilities as fathers. The startling statistics keep the organizations motivated.

One such organization is FamilyLife. According to research this organization reported in an article in its magazine *RealFamilyLife*, about 40 percent of American children go to bed each night in homes where their fathers do not live. By the time children reach the age of eighteen, more than half are likely to have spent at least a portion of their childhoods apart from their fathers.[7]

The article goes on to report that fatherless children are more likely to drop out of school, become involved in crime, and commit suicide. They are more frequent targets of sexual abuse and they are more likely to have children out of wedlock.

"Never before in this country have so many children been voluntarily abandoned by their fathers. Never before have so many children grown up without knowing what it means to have a father," said David Blankenhorn of the Institute for American Values in the article titled, "Where Are the Fathers?"[8]

Those are the fathers who are *physically* absent. Harder to measure statistically, but equally devastating to children, is the increase in the number of *emotionally* absent dads.

Sociologists trace the problem of passive fathers back to when men began leaving their farms to go work in office buildings and factories. It was then that many men began to define fathering simply as breadwinning and left parenting to their wives. Other factors contributing to this change of attitude toward fatherhood included the feminist movement, the confusion of gender roles, and the advent of other demands on a man's time. "With this kind of uninvolved father," writes Tony Evans, Jr., pastor of Oak Cliff Bible Fellowship in Dallas, "what we are getting is a generation of children being raised on the world's values."[9]

Another organization dedicated to equipping fathers is The National Center for Fathering, founded by author and speaker Ken Canfield, Ph.D., and his associates in 1990. The organization's mission is to strengthen fathers and champion the role of fathering to this generation. It believes that turning fathers' hearts to their children is a vital part of helping our culture regain its sense of family. It also publishes a magazine for fathers titled *Today's Father: For Men Who Want to Be Better Dads*, full of practical advice to dads on how to get more involved in their kids' lives.

It's often said that the best thing a father can do for his children is love their mother. Promise Keepers is an organization dedicated to helping fathers do just that in homes across America.

The organization was founded by Bill McCartney, then head coach of the University of Colorado football team. Standing on the sidelines for all those years watching screaming fans inspired McCartney's dream to fill a stadium with men who were turned on for Jesus Christ instead. He did it.

What began as a discussion with a friend on a long car ride resulted in 4,200 men gathering for the first Promise Keepers Conference in July of 1991. Now more than 3.2 million men have attended these stadium events nationwide.

The feminist press came out in opposition to Promise Keepers when the group held its massive "Stand in the Gap" rally in Washington, D.C. in October 1997. Misunderstanding the Promise Keepers' support of the biblical principles of submission, they labeled the group oppressive to women. Nothing could be further from the truth. What non-believing women don't understand is that Christian men are called to love their wives "just as Christ loved the church and gave himself up for her" (Eph. 5:25). There is no greater love.

Promise #4 of the Seven Promises of a Promise Keeper states: A promise keeper is committed to building strong marriages and families through love, protection, and biblical values.

Many women celebrate the changes in husbands who have attended a Promise Keeper event or joined one of the small group studies the organization sponsors in neighborhoods across America. Positive changes. That's why nearly 65 percent of the one thousand volunteers who put on each conference are women. "Yes!" These women are saying. "I want a Promise Keeper for a husband, and for the father of my children." The feminists protest because women are not included in the event. Why would they *want* to go when they can send their husbands and reap the benefits?

An editorial writer in *USA Today* responded to the feminist criticism by researching reactions of wives whose husbands had gone to Promise Keepers.

"Where is my husband?" wrote Lori Day of Springfield, Missouri. "He didn't come home from the Promise Keepers conference in Dallas. A man came back who *looked* like my husband but he didn't act like my husband. I don't want my old husband to return—I love my new husband's actions and attitudes. I wish every wife could have a Promise Keeper husband."[10]

When NOW protestors claimed Promise Keepers was sending out a "misogynistic message" that says "men must take back control of the family, be the head, the boss," they missed the part that says the men are to be servant leaders to their wives and children, much as Jesus washed the feet of those who followed him.

The writer of the editorial concluded, "Perhaps this explains why a recent study found that the men most likely to help their wives with household chores are orthodox Christians who believe the Bible is God's word and the answer to all important human problems." [11]

The Value of Submission

How can a wife help her husband be a better father? By accepting that he is different from her and will view parenting differently. By acknowledging his need to be respected and encouraged by her. And yes, by submitting to his leadership in the home, especially his spiritual leadership.

"It is not good for the man to be alone," God said in Genesis 2:18. "I will make a helper suitable for him." God's recognized need for man to have a helper-completer gave birth to the role He wants women to fill within the marriage relationship. Many women shy away from this role because they don't see it as equally important to the role of male leadership—but God does. He created women to be the very crown of creation, created for holy purposes with eternal significance—purposes every bit as valuable in His eyes as those He gives to men. But different. When a wife refuses to fulfill her role as helper-completer, maybe even choosing to compete with her husband rather than complete him, both she and her husband may find that their marriage is far less than God intended.

A wife's reticence to accept her helper-completer role is often fueled by the fact that our society demands equality in every situation. She is looking at her assignment in the world's eyes, not God's. If she sees being a helper-completer as a submissive role, she may reject it. The same woman who finds structure in the workplace acceptable and necessary may find it deplorable that God has a similar strategic plan for organizing a family that works—but He does.

As mentioned earlier, Ephesians, chapter 5, is the place most people turn to hear God's plan for submission. In Ephesians 5:21, all believers are told to "submit to one another out of reverence for Christ." Wives are instructed to "submit to their husbands in everything" (Eph. 5:24), while husbands are instructed to love their wives "just as Christ loved the church" (Eph. 5:25). It's easy for a wife to submit when she is loved like that!

Still, the Bible passage that helps me most in submitting to my husband is found in Philippians 2:5-8: "Your attitude should be the same as that of Christ Jesus: Who, being in very nature God, did not consider equality with God something to be grasped, but made himself nothing, taking the very nature of a servant, being made in human likeness. And being found in appearance as a man, he humbled himself and became obedient to death—even death on a cross!"

If Jesus Christ could submit for the good of humanity, I can submit for the good of my family, resting in the comfort that by grace I am equally loved along with all the saints in God's eyes. The model we have for submission is the model of the Trinity itself. Jesus is submissive to the Father. The Holy Spirit gives glory to Jesus. But all three are equally divine.

Longfellow gave a poetic twist to submission when he wrote:

As unto the bow the cord is,
So unto the man is woman,
Though she bends him, she obeys him,
Though she draws him, yet she follows,
Useless each without the other!

Perhaps no analogy so beautifully captures the successful blending of leadership and submission in marriage as the sport of ice dancing. Perfectly in tune with each other, he leads and she follows. Mutual trust and communication are essential. He is strong enough to lift her up, but she is able to stay balanced and can land on her own two feet gracefully at any time. In perfect harmony, they glide through their dance, creating something far grander than either of them could create alone.

It is a wise mom who sees the healthy role submission plays in keeping a home intact with both a mom and a dad in residence. And it's a wise dad who values his wife's counsel and her unique position of respect in the home.

In Defense of Dads

Women know how valuable dads are. Children know it too. That's why it's so confounding to see the father's role in the home being undervalued and dismissed as superfluous by some professionals in our society.

Columnist Suzanne Fields responded loudly when Frank Furstenburg, a sociologist at the University of Pennsylvania who has been studying fathers for twenty years, concluded that we don't know why, or even if, fathers really matter. The columnist's own experience in interviewing women and girls across America on their memories of their fathers told her otherwise.

"Mature women lined up to tell me both sad and wonderful stories of remembering daddy," Fields said. "The absent father still brought tears to their eyes. Social science will never measure the pain of a boy and girl who have no father to introduce to their friends."

Fields quotes results from a psychological study of white, lower middle-class daughters between the ages of thirteen and seventeen. The study concluded that "adolescent girls growing up without fathers felt less personal control over their lives, and had more difficulty dealing with males of the species."[12]

The next study to confound those who know the value of the father in the home was released by none other than The American Psychological Association. The APA released results of a study in 1999 that essentially declared the dad obsolete, suggesting that fathers and even marriage are unnecessary for healthy child development.

In the report, titled "Deconstructing the American Father," Louise Silverstein and Carl Auerbach claimed fathers do not make a "unique and essential contribution to child development."[13]

Chuck Colson, former special counsel to President Nixon and founder of Prison Fellowship, didn't let news reports of this study go by without rebuttal. Stating that "the evidence pointing to the importance of fathers is overwhelming," Colson supported his defense with statistics to tell the real story.

Based on his own experience and research in prisons, Colson argued that boys who grow up without their fathers are at least twice as likely as other boys to end up in prison. Sixty percent of rapists and 72 percent of adolescent murderers never knew or lived with their fathers. And Colson says the ill effects of life without a father present are not limited to any one class, race, or sex. In fact, his statistics reveal that affluent white girls raised without a father are five times more likely to become mothers while still adolescents.

"Of course, intact traditional families have problems, too," Colson concludes. "But only someone blinded by a political agenda would not see that they're the best environment for children . . . human fathers, like our heavenly One, are irreplaceable."[14]

Surely common sense will win out in the end and the value of a father to a family, to a home, will go unquestioned once again.

In 1996, The National Fatherhood Initiative joined with the Ad Council to sponsor a full-page ad in *USA Today*. On the left side of the page was a headline reading, "What it takes to be a father." Under the headline was a photograph of a sperm under a microscope.

But on the right-hand side of the page, under the headline, "What it takes to be a dad," was a list of twenty-seven things a father who wants to be a real dad can do. Things like: Read to your children. Keep your promises. Set a good example. Show your children lots of warmth and affection. Take your children to work. Take your children to your place of worship. Fly a kite together.

It's true that anyone can be a father, but it takes someone special to be a dad. It's equally true that a home with a dad is a home where children have the best chance of growing up well-adjusted and emotionally whole.

"No man has ever lived that had enough of children's gratitude or woman's love," William Butler Yeats wrote. A real dad receives both, and the children and woman who live in a home with him as the father-in-residence are blessed indeed.

♡ Home Builders:

1. What similarities, if any, do you see between your father's character and God's character?
2. The most effective fathers are physically and emotionally available to their children. List specific signs a father is truly present for his children.
3. Whether or not your father is still alive, write a letter to him thanking him for any positive ways in which he affected your life.

A Home Unlatched

· · · · · · · · · · · · · · · ·

A small house well filled is
better than an empty palace.

—*Thomas D. Haliburton*

I s a family home that stands empty from 7:30 in the morning until 6:00 in the evening really a home, or is it only a house? The only sounds are the slow drip, drip, drip of a faucet leaking into a sink full of dirty dishes and the tick, tick, tick of the mantle clock in the living room. A cat stares into an empty food bowl and wonders why no one notices it's empty. A dog shivers by the back door and wonders why no one lets him in. When there are no people present, a house is not a home; it's just a house.

Adults who come home to an empty house after working all day still feel a sense of welcome when they walk through the door, but coming in to an empty house isn't a satisfying experience for a child. How I wish I understood this as clearly when my boys were small. I was rarely home alone then, so I never imagined what our home would be like with no one else there. I didn't understand how it would feel for the boys to walk into a house instead of a home. I just knew I had to be at work, and whatever else had to take place in order to make that happen, so be it.

When I first began to work full time after my divorce, I tried an after-school baby-sitter. But the day I came home to find her doing her nails and talking on the phone while my boys entertained themselves, I decided I was wasting my resources on baby-sitting.

When I talked the situation over with the boys, I heard what I wanted to hear; I heard what was most convenient for me. They were anxious to try being home alone. I chose to believe the experts who said "independent time" was character building for children. After a trip to the key shop for extra house keys on chains to wear around their necks, two more latchkey children, ages eight and eleven, entered the world.

They weren't alone. Research from that period indicates that at least six million children in the United States were in "self care" for some part of each day in the early '80s, most in the eight-to-thirteen age range. By 1998, that number was up to seven million and growing.[1]

Whereas most of those kids are only home alone for an average of two hours a day during the school year, a new dilemma arises when school is out for the summer. Should they then be left alone all day? At what cost? What risk is too great a risk to take? In many states, it is illegal to leave a child younger than twelve home alone, but it happens all the time.

In the 1991 movie *Home Alone,* eight-year-old Kevin outsmarts a pair of burglars who invade his home. For Kevin, being home alone is just one big adventure. Most children in Kevin's shoes would have felt much differently.

It was years before I understood how my children were affected by the latchkey experience. It pains me to think that even as I write this, some parent somewhere is deciding the time is right to let her own children try being alone after school. Like all of us before her, this parent is focusing on all the positive, valid reasons for having children in self care. I know what they are. I wrote the book.

I'm Home/Be Home Soon

What better way could I have justified my own decision to leave my children at home unsupervised than to write a book proclaiming the virtues of self care? Working for a publisher, Current, Inc., permitted me that privilege.

I'm Home/Be Home Soon was actually two books in one, with a fill-in-the-blank section in the middle that parents and children could complete together to come up with a "super plan" contract.[2] The book sold well through the Current catalog, and it received endorsements from the director of Parents Without Partners, and the national vice-president of NOW (National Organization for Women). Churches, Girl Scout troops, and school districts wrote to say they were using it in training programs for latchkey children.

The *I'm Home* section of the book is written to kids and tells them what it means (from an adult perspective, of course) to be a latchkey kid. It talks about telephone etiquette, doing chores, dealing with strangers at the door, and other emergencies. It also gives advice on caring for pets and getting along with brothers and sisters. It even includes simple snack recipes and some first-aid tips recommended by the American Red Cross.

The *Be Home Soon* section of the book covers all the same issues from the parents' point of view. It discusses making the decision for self care, networking with other parents, keeping in touch with the school, caring for a sick child, creating a safe environment, the sibling situation, and more.

If the book helped children make the best of a bad situation, I'm glad. If it encouraged parents to opt to leave their children home alone when they had other viable choices for child care, I wish I hadn't written it.

Looking back through a fifteen-year-old file of responses to the book, I find only one negative letter. In this scathing attack written on lined notebook paper, a stay-at-home mom named Donna accused my company of selling feminist propaganda.

"This 'self care' is really an 'I don't care' attitude of parents— especially mothers," she wrote. She went on to say that latchkey children are really neglected children, and that neglect equals abuse. "There *are* latchkey children and they *do* have problems," she continued, "but the answer is not a book on how to cope, it's a book on how mom can stay at home and take care of these children as she was meant to do."

No one, least of all me, took Donna's letter seriously when it arrived—not even the part of the letter where she went on to threaten a boycott against my company. After all, this was a pressing social issue, and we were addressing it responsibly. The research and endorsements all confirmed that we were doing the right thing.

Then why did I save Donna's letter for so long? Could it be because, even as I self-righteously basked in the warm reception the book received, something in my mother's heart whispered that she was right?

Recent studies confirm that, in fact, children left in self care are vulnerable to more than the obvious dangers. Perhaps worse than a dangerous stranger at the door, or walking into a house that has been burglarized, are the longer-lasting ill effects of lack of adult supervision.

A study by social scientist Jean L. Richardson revealed that eighth grade students who took care of themselves for eleven or more hours a week were twice as likely to smoke marijuana or drink alcohol as those who were actively cared for by adults.[3]

I wish I had known that before I put a key around the neck of my older son, Rob. I wish I had known before he dropped out of high school three times and was finally committed to a thirty-day drug rehabilitation program in a local hospital.

Proverbs 29:13 says, "a child left to himself disgraces his mother." I certainly felt disgraced sitting in the counselor's office one afternoon while Rob was still in the program. I listened as my son explained that whereas I wasn't around for him to talk to, his pot-smoking, beer-guzzling friends were. Even as I felt these words twisting like a knife in my chest, I still didn't connect Rob's problems with my ill-conceived decision for self care. I could have made other arrangements financially. Accepting all the child support the courts said I was entitled to would have allowed me to keep working part time and be home in the afternoon. Instead, I pridefully told my ex-husband I could get by on less, then accepted a promotion and full-time position.

Not only had I decided on self care for my own children, I had written a book that might lead some other mother to have to endure a similar afternoon in some other counselor's office.

A Look at the Dangers

The dangers are so obvious that I don't know how I could have ignored them. For instance, most responsible parents with children home alone have rules. One rule is that the kids, especially teenagers, may not have friends in the house. How do teenagers get around that rule? Simple. If their friends can't come to them, then they go to their friends. Essentially, we liberated working moms of the '80s forced our teenagers out into the streets. All the studies confirm that the more time a teenager remains unsupervised, the greater the risk. (Do we really need studies to tell us that?)

Child care legislation advocates and I have different motivations for alerting parents to the hazards of leaving kids unsupervised. They hope to motivate taxpayers to fund government day-care programs, whereas I'm more interested in encouraging parents to work out ways to be at home with their kids. But we agree on the end result.

However misguided her political ideology, Hillary Rodham Clinton, in her book *It Takes a Village,* makes a valid observation: "Whether they are middle-class 'latchkey kids', ghetto kids, or kids whose parents are too wrapped up in their own lives to pay attention to them, they are raising themselves, like the band of stranded schoolboys in *Lord of the Flies,"* she wrote. "And in the absence of parental guidance, children turn to other authority or pseudo-authority figures—to gang leaders, to older children who are also adrift, and to the dubious role models popular culture provides."[4]

Additionally, teachers and law enforcement officials alike confirm that lack of parental supervision at home is a major contributing factor to violence in schools. Involvement in crime, early sexual experimentation, and the teenage pregnancies that result are also decidedly more prevalent in the latchkey population.

Of course not all latchkey kids wind up in drug rehabilitation programs or under arrest. Many truly will be more responsible and independent because they were forced to care for themselves. But being responsible at the age of eight has its own drawbacks.

Enter my second son, Tim.

One day I picked up the phone at work and was surprised when a teller at a bank near our house told me that my son, then nine, was trying to open a savings account. "Do you know his social security number?" she asked matter-of-factly.

I told this story for years as an example of how independent and advanced in years my son was. It always got a laugh or two. Now when I think about that same story, I just want to cry.

Tim had gotten checks from his grandparents for his birthday and he wanted to open a bank account. Where was the parent who would explain the principles of banking to him and take him to the bank? Why did he decide that his only course of action was to put on his Cub Scout uniform and ride his bike to the closest bank? Why did I think that was cute, rather than sad?

It's now known that even the latchkey kids who develop independent thinking skills and good self-esteem often have long-lasting feelings of abandonment, and may be haunted into adulthood by a need to overachieve, or a need to be in control of every situation. Perfectionism runs rampant in this population. They weren't allowed to be children when they were children, so they spend their young adulthood proving they have no tolerance for "childish" ways. It's a different kind of tragic aftereffect.

In the classic codependency model, when one child in a family acts out, another may take on the role of "family hero" in order to prove to the world that the family is okay after all. Tim became our hero in all the ways the world measures: president of the National Honor Society, member of a championship tennis team, acceptance to Northwestern University. These were achievements Tim earned for himself, but we all basked in his glory.

I do believe Tim would have excelled in spite of his situation at home, but I'm left wondering if he will suffer any long-term effects from the extra pressure he felt to be in control at such a young age. Gratefully, he survived his over-achieving years just as his older brother survived his troubled ones. He learned to have fun in life all over again, and after graduating from Princeton Seminary, is now enjoying his job as associate pastor of a Presbyterian church in New Jersey. I'm always pleased when I hear that in addition to the serious preaching and pastoring Tim does, he makes time to have fun with his wife and daughter, and with the junior high kids in his youth group. He's still a hero, but for all the right reasons these days.

All this is to say the arrangements we make as parents for the care of our children can have a lifelong impact on them. Each of us has her own baggage to carry in life. But when we give our children a particularly heavy duffel bag to tote, we need to be aware of what we're doing. It's a fact that some of those bags come with latchkeys attached.

When There's No Choice

I must emphasize here that I know many women, especially single moms, have absolutely no choice other than to leave their children home alone. If you are in this position, I understand. Ask the Lord to protect your children. Put safeguards in place, be alert to signs of problems, and you will survive. "As a mother comforts her child, so will I comfort you," the Lord says in Isaiah 66:13. Throughout the Bible He promises to protect orphans (even temporary ones!) and widows and to be a husband to the husbandless. "For the Maker is your husband—the Lord Almighty is his name—the Holy One of Israel is your Redeemer; he is called the God of all the earth" says Isaiah 54:5. Claim those verses, believe them, and be renewed by them daily.

I'm truly glad there are wonderful systems set up to help parents and kids in latchkey situations. Volunteers staff "warm lines" like the one in Chicago called "Grandma, Please!" Latchkey children can call the "warm line" when they feel the need to hear an adult voice or want some help with their homework.

Many churches and community organizations like the YMCA offer after-school programs at little or no cost in addition to providing parents of latchkey children with resources and helplines. If you must leave your children unsupervised, don't hesitate to take advantage of these services.

Also, don't be too proud to ask another parent to pick up your child for soccer practice if you can't be home in time, or to ask a neighbor to be available for emergencies. You can always bring the kids home after practice and return the favor to your neighbor on the weekend. If your best-laid plans aren't working and you know you need to make some changes, make some phone calls. Ask coworkers what arrangements they have made. Surf that strongest of networks: Mom.net!

Even though I wish I'd never written a book outlining how to set up a workable plan for self care, it does help to establish rules about what children may and may not do after school. There are guidelines you can establish which decrease the anxiety for you and your kids.

It's a good thing to establish phone contact every afternoon, and it helps to leave notes on the kitchen counter or tuck love notes in lunch boxes for your kids to find during the day.

It even helps to have a pet. When my boys were home alone, I found comfort in the statistic that a pet relieves 75 percent of the loneliness of coming home to an empty house. We had a golden retriever. I wonder why it didn't occur to me that by relying on that statistic, I was saying that I could be replaced by a dog!

But even with all these Band-Aids in place, investigate all other possibilities before deciding you have no other option than to leave your children home alone. Is there a neighbor who would willingly include your kids with her own around the kitchen table after school? What about a grandma, aunt, sister, or friend who would welcome a chance to build a real relationship with your children? Maybe two or more relatives could alternate days.

When a critical piece of your decision to put your children into self care is the financial one, I invite you to challenge your own suppositions about how much money you really need. Put pencil to paper. Separate needs from wants, and explore embracing the concept that less really can be more, and enough is quite often truly enough.

The Bible provides many reassuring verses about how the Lord will continue to provide for our needs when we are concerned about how to keep a roof over our children's heads. "Even the sparrow has found a home," we read, "and the swallow a nest for herself, where she may have her young—a place near your altar, O Lord Almighty, my King and my God" (Ps. 84:3).

Homes We Remember

Have you ever had the experience of going back to a childhood home and realizing that it is much smaller and less imposing than you remember it being as a child? We need to console ourselves if our homes seem too small or lack the amenities we would like for our children to have. What they will remember about home has less to do with the color of the carpet or the size of the rooms than with the memories they made sharing the space with their families and a few truly remarkable pets.

A friend of mine tells a wonderful story about taking her husband and two teenagers back to a suburb of Chicago so they could see where she lived as a young child. As they turned the corner onto her old street, her heart started beating faster and tears formed in her eyes.

"Oh look!" she said when the three-story, brick townhouse came into view. "I used to play under that bay window creating little villages in the dirt."

The family excitedly got out of their rental car and walked up the front steps to ring the doorbell. An elderly woman came to the door. When my friend explained how she wanted her husband and children to see her childhood home, the woman graciously invited them in. So pleased was the resident to share the history of the house that she led them on a two-hour tour from room to room, giving a running narrative of her own paintings and belongings along the way.

Finally, the family said their good-byes and thank-yous and climbed back into the car.

That's when my friend's husband looked at her and said, "That wasn't it, was it?"

"No, it wasn't," she confessed.

"When did you know?" he asked.

"Oh, about ten minutes into the tour," she said, "but by then I didn't want to disappoint that sweet old woman!"

When they finally located the real site on the next corner, they just waved and drove on past. Meanwhile, my friend enjoyed her childhood memories every bit as much as if they had been in the right house! The place doesn't matter nearly as much as the memories, and sometimes the simplest homes are the best places to raise children.

Claire Cloninger wrote a wonderful book about simplifying life titled *A Place Called Simplicity.* In it, she tells about the decision she and her husband made to sell their big, expensive house in the city and move to a riverside cabin.

"The homes that I enjoy the most have less to do with architecture and décor and more to do with authenticity," she wrote. "A home feels simple and unified and whole to me when it speaks with the accents of the people who live there. A home that expresses the character, tastes, and values of the people who live in it is authentic whether it be sleek and modern, rustic and homey, ruffled and charming, or spare and graceful."[5]

Claire and her husband simplified in many ways besides moving to a smaller house, including getting out of debt and learning to live more richly with less.

"The further we go on this journey toward a simpler financial life, the more people we become aware of who are moving in the same direction," Cloninger writes. "It seems that many of us, in our individual ways, are fighting back—turning off the television commercials and cutting up the credit cards. . . . We are refusing to let our lives be defined by our addresses or our automobiles or the brand new name on our jeans."[6]

In the book I wrote about my own simplification journey, *Simply the Savior*, I talk about how I asked the Lord to take away my desire to acquire. He did. He'll be happy to help you learn to live with less, too, especially if it means you'll be able to arrange your work schedule to be home when the kids aren't in school.

Facing the Truth

If you're sure you have no other choice for child care, and you're absolutely sure you can't survive without the income from a full-time salary, make the best of the latchkey situation. If you do have a choice, think carefully before leaving children of any age home alone. I say this in hopes of sparing you one of the greatest regrets I have as a parent: I didn't give my children the same homecoming experiences I had as a child.

I remember the times my mother was not at home to greet me after school only because they were so few as to be memorable. Even when she wasn't there, I was greeted warmly. My grandmother, who lived with us, would fix me peanut butter toast and pour me a big glass of milk, then listen patiently to me as I talked about my day.

I don't think I saw the whole truth about my decision to put my sons in self care until several years ago when I was in a Bible study focusing on the roles of women. In horror I read about fallen women in the Bible who planned to eat their children (Deut. 28:56-57), or burn them as sacrifices to false gods (Jer. 7:31). My horror was magnified when I realized that women who emotionally or physically turn away from their God-given nurturing roles, also sacrifice their children to false gods. The only difference is, the gods they worship are the gods of convenience, economic independence, pride, or materialism. Coming face-to-face with that truth made me realize that I had nearly sacrificed my children to those same false gods.

Sadly, such sacrificing goes on and on. In her book *The Time Bind,* sociologist Arlie Hochschild infuriated many feminists by suggesting that personal comfort rather than economic need is the driving force behind the growing numbers of children separated from their mothers during the day. Women, she says, find the orderly workplace to be a more nurturing place than a home filled with drudge work and unruly children. Besides, she adds, the modest homes that used to be populated by stay-at-home moms have been replaced by manses requiring two incomes to finance.[7] Are such homes truly a "need"?

By the grace of God, both of my sons survived their latchkey experiences, and have grown up to be college graduates, happily married husbands, and caring fathers. I asked them to forgive me for those "home alone" years, and they have.

Blessedly, I also know I have God's forgiveness for my short-sightedness, and I praise Him for being a vigilant parent when I was not. Not only did He forgive me, but He also took away my guilt. Were that not so, I would never have been able to write this book.

Like the women in the Bible who brought life to their families by drawing water from the well, we can bring life to ours by asking the Lord to help us make the decisions that impact the lives of our children. And when we are tired and thirsty, the Lord who provides "a spring of water welling up to eternal life" will refresh and sustain us (John 4:14).

Having a parent at home does matter to a child. My friend Pat, now in her fifties, remembers the difference it makes. "My mother worked when I was in junior high and high school back in the '60s," she told me. "Not everyone's mother did work outside the home back then, although it was becoming more the norm. I was very involved in many activities in high school and I remember we had a creative writing class that met three days a week after school. I was there every time—unless my mom had a day off work. On the days I knew she would be home, I wanted to be home too. Just knowing she would be there made going home a totally different, suddenly inviting prospect."

Go before the Lord and ask Him to help you choose His will for your family. If you have a latchkey child, and if it is at all possible, take the key from around your child's neck. Whether it's a humble little dwelling or a palace, make your house a home: an unlatched home with a big hug waiting on the other side of the door.

♡ Home Builders:

1. What emotions do you associate with coming home? How do they differ now from when you were a child?
2. If you are the mother of a latchkey child, how might you ease the situation or provide a sense of security and connectedness for your child when you can't be there?
3. There may be a latchkey family on your street or in your neighborhood. If so, how might you help them to create a better homecoming experience for their children? Please try.

A Home with Boundaries

• • • • • • • • • • • • • •

The duties of home are discipline
for the ministries of heaven.

—*Anonymous*

L et's face it. Some parts of parenting are just more fun than others. It's fun to finger paint with your toddler. It's not fun to listen to her cry when she is sent to her room for smearing blue and green paint on the new white sofa.

It's fun to take your teenager down to the driver's license bureau to take his driver's test and to see the ecstatic look of pride and joy on his face when he finds out he passed. It's not fun to sit up until 1:30 in the morning waiting to hear the garage door go up, hearing sirens blaring in the night, and worrying that your child and your car may be lost forever. It's also not fun to have the discussion that will result in your taking the car keys away because he broke curfew. Again.

And yet, like so many jobs we get stuck with as adults, when it comes to parenting, we have to take the bad with the good. While disciplining our children may not be as enjoyable as playing ball with them, we have to do it if we are to have homes that provide a sanctuary for everyone in the family and produce well-adjusted adults.

My husband and I have often been caught off guard, and left social gatherings aghast, by what seems to be the total lack of common sense that can come over otherwise sane people once they become parents. For some reason, this malady seems especially evident in those who have children late in life. We really do try to be understanding and refrain from judging others engaged in the hardest job on earth, but we scratch our heads when otherwise accomplished, clear-thinking adults just seem to check out when it comes to disciplining their young children.

For example, we were enjoying a wonderful meal in one home when the couple's toddler crawled across the formal white tablecloth and dipped her hand into each crystal glass of ice water. The parents thought it was cute.

Talking to another couple on the phone late one night, my husband heard their two-year-old son crying in the background. "What time does he usually go to bed?" he asked, thinking the child must be sick to be up so late. "He doesn't really go to bed," was the answer. "We just wait until he falls asleep somewhere on the floor and then we carry him upstairs."

Another time we were told we couldn't do dinner and a movie with friends because their three year old wouldn't stay more than an hour-and-a-half at a time with the grandparents who offered to baby-sit him. What did they mean he wouldn't stay with his grandparents? What did he do, call a cab?

All these situations are summed up nicely in a "Close to Home" cartoon by artist John McPherson. In the drawing, a man and woman are confined in a playpen while a toddler sits with the remote control watching TV. The caption reads, "At the age of only fifteen months, Jason was already a master of reverse psychology."

The greatest disservice we can do to our children is to give them control of our homes and families. They don't have the skills and mental development necessary to call all the shots; yet that's what many parents are asking their children to do when, locked in the bind of discipline avoidance, they give in to every whim their children have. In essence, they reverse positions with their children and say, "You run the household. We'll just sit here ready to react to whatever you decide to do."

One of our jobs as parents is to develop clear thinking in our children. We can't do that by asking them to make decisions they aren't equipped to make. Another couple we know goes into a long negotiation session with their toddler over where the child will sleep each night. "Do you want to sleep in your bed or in mommy and daddy's bed?" they ask. The child usually just falls to the floor in a full-fledged, screaming tantrum. If he could express himself better, he might say, "Isn't it supposed to be your job to decide where I sleep? After all, you two are the adults around here."

We're fond of all of these people and realize that the years may have clouded our memories of similar mistakes we may have made when our own children were small. Also, having children in our early twenties meant that we weren't that far removed from our own parents' authority. Maybe it was easier for us to imitate what we saw our parents doing than it is for first-time parents in their forties. But how do we explain the reticence of some younger parents to discipline their children, too?

This problem of discipline avoidance by parents may stem from lack of understanding of two principles so clear in Scripture: "all have sinned and fall short of the glory of God" (Rom. 3:23) and "in this world you will have trouble" (John 16:33). Understanding the first helps parents realize that the babies they bring home from the hospital are not as innocent and perfect as they look, but are filled with the same tendencies toward selfishness, defiance, and rebellion that lurk within every human. Understanding the second helps them accept that it's okay for children to cry. It's our job as parents to help our kids understand that things won't always go their way in life. And it's better that they learn this at age two rather than leaving it for the marriage counselor to address when they are forty-two.

Discipline vs. Punishment

There must be as many theories about how to discipline children as there are remedies for a colicky baby, but the experts seem to agree that discipline must be done out of love if it is to be a positive influence in a child's life rather than a negative one. They also agree that discipline and punishment are not one in the same. While both may be appropriate at times, the confusion between the two may keep parents from engaging in either.

Dr. James Dobson is recognized worldwide as an expert on raising children effectively and compassionately. His first book, *Dare to Discipline,* published in 1970, was an instant success and sold more than two million copies in twenty years. In 1992, *The New Dare to Discipline* was published. Still based on the traditional Judeo-Christian system of values that helps parents achieve a balance between love and control, the revised book adheres to Dobson's basic principles, while updating examples and context to reflect current social issues.

"I am not suggesting that you insulate your dignity and authority by being cold and unapproachable," Dr. Dobson states. "These parental tactics do not produce healthy, responsible children. By contrast, I am recommending a simple principle: when you are defiantly challenged, win decisively. When the child asks 'Who's in charge?' tell him. When he mutters 'Who loves me?' take him in your arms and surround him with affection. Treat him with respect and dignity, and expect the same from him. Then begin to enjoy the sweet benefits of competent parenthood."[1]

Isn't that really the issue here? In homes where toddlers and pre-schoolers are in charge, or teenagers are driving the family schedule, the parents are not enjoying being parents. Furthermore, they have little to no time to be together as a married couple because all of their time and energy is spent reacting to the children they appointed masters of the home.

Why are these parents, and so many others, abdicating their responsibility to discipline their children? Again, it may be because they confuse discipline with punishment.

One mom and I were visiting in her kitchen as her toddler roamed around getting into cupboards, taking food out and eating it, generally doing whatever his little heart desired.

"I don't ever want to say no to him unless he is hurting himself or others," the mom explained. "I've even told the sitter who comes in to care for him during the day never to use the word no around him. It's just too negative." Needless to say, this couple went through quite a few sitters before finding one who agreed with their philosophy of parenting. Because they didn't understand that discipline isn't the same thing as punishment, they didn't discipline.

Dr. Dobson turns to another expert, reality therapist William Glasser, to explain the difference. According to Glasser, discipline is directed at objectional behavior, and the child will accept its consequence without resentment. Punishment is a response that is directed at the individual. It represents a desire of one person to hurt another, and it is an expression of hostility rather than corrective love. As such, it is often deeply resented by the child.[2]

The book *Boundaries,* by clinical psychologists Dr. Henry Cloud and Dr. John Townsend, also speaks to the distinction between punishment and discipline. Punishment is payment for wrongdoing, the authors state, and doesn't leave much room for mistakes. It deals with something that happened in the past.

"Discipline, however, is different," Cloud and Townsend write. "Discipline is not punishment for a wrong. It's the natural law of God: our actions reap consequences."[3]

Such discipline is best administered by loving parents in control.

"Much has been written about the dangers of harsh, oppressive, unloving discipline; these warnings are valid and should be heeded," Dr. Dobson writes. "However, the consequences of oppressive discipline have been cited as justification for the abdication of leadership. That is foolish. There are times when a strong-willed child will clench his little fists and dare his parents to accept his challenges. He is not motivated by frustration or inner hostility, as it is often supposed. He merely wants to know where the boundaries lie and who's available to enforce them."[4]

It takes a home with consistent discipline and clear, immutable boundaries for a child to grow up secure in who he or she is in this world. Wise parents understand and teach the principles of self-protection, limit setting, delayed gratification, and responsibility. They nurture children to have a sense of control and choice, and to respect the limits of others in the family.

God's Boundaries

Why are boundaries so actively avoided? Like a cowboy singing the old Cole Porter song of the '30s, we seem to be a whole nation of people singing "don't fence me in." When did we forget that fences also keep harm and confusion from moving in on the world in which we live, love, and raise our children?

Parents need only look to the example of God's creation to see that boundaries are a natural part of the world He created, and a necessary part of a godly home.

In the beginning, God created the sea and the dry land. Each is vast in scope and rich in bounty to be discovered. But the place where the two meet is a natural boundary that can't be denied. Sea-dwelling creatures that find themselves washed ashore outside of the boundary will soon die for lack of water. Land-dwelling creatures who find themselves adrift under the ocean with no oxygen source to sustain them will also perish. God created a boundary that, without artificial intervention, we cannot violate.

"He marks out the horizon on the face of the waters for a boundary between light and darkness," we read in Job 26:10.

And what about the boundary God established when he placed Adam and Eve in the Garden of Eden? "You are free to eat from any tree in the garden; but you must not eat from the tree of the knowledge of good and evil, for when you eat of it you will surely die," God told Adam in Genesis 2:16-17. You know the rest of the story. Adam told Eve what God had said, then Eve told the serpent, but the serpent convinced Eve to ignore God's boundary. Eve then convinced Adam to do the same.

In Genesis 3 we see the consequences. First God cursed the serpent, telling him that someone was going to come through the woman who would crush Satan and win the battle for the human race. Blessedly, that someone was Jesus Christ.

But then God cursed Eve, and told her she would have pain in childbirth and that her "desire will be for her husband"—the phrase Barbara Mouser and other scholars interpret not as sexual or psychological dependence, but as the desire a woman has to rule her husband. Women today still suffer under both aspects of the curse as we give birth and as we struggle with what it really means to be submissive to our husband's leadership.

God also cursed Adam, telling him he would encounter many obstacles in his work.

Adam and Eve were then banished from the Garden forever, "and he placed on the east side of the Garden of Eden cherubim and a flaming sword flashing back and forth to guard the way to the tree of life" (Gen. 3:24). God doesn't take it lightly when His boundaries are ignored. There will be consequences.

There's another garden God created with specific boundaries. One so private and special, so secure and protected that it's the workshop He chooses for the continuation of His creation. This garden doesn't have stone walls or trellises, but it contains the very fountain of life. It is the womb of the woman.

The Song of Solomon describes lovemaking as the husband entering the garden, his wife. In Song of Solomon 5:1, the husband says, "I have come into my garden, my sister, my bride; I have gathered my myrrh along with my spice. I have eaten my honeycomb and my honey; I have drunk my wine and my milk." There aren't many romance novels that get steamier than that! In Song of Solomon 4:12, the garden of her virginity is described this way: "You are a garden locked up, my sister, my bride; you are a spring enclosed, a sealed fountain." The joy the husband feels is heightened by the knowledge that his wife's body was a locked garden until she permitted him to enter it.

So one of the boundaries God set up from the beginning was the wall He wanted around the virgin's womb. Have there been consequences involved in the violation of this boundary? Of course.

Television sitcoms may be influencing the moral decline of our society, but in fairness they also reflect what's happening to people in real life. Watch for ten minutes or so, and you'll clearly hear the message that virginity is not a secret garden to be locked up, but rather something a young woman should lose as quickly and recklessly as possible. The effect such behavior will have on the womb is not considered at all. Certainly the womb is not considered to be God's sacred workshop.

And the consequences? Where shall we begin? Sexually transmitted disease, abortion, and fatherless children surely top the list. But what about loss of a young woman's self-esteem, her modesty, and the sacred trust implicit in her ability to give life? How do we assess those losses?

"The virginity of a nation's women, their purity, is one of the greatest natural and human resources that we have, because virginity is a gateway to two things of monumental importance," Barbara Mouser writes in her study *Five Aspects of Woman*. "First, it is the gateway to a woman's capacity to love a man, and second, to a woman's capacity to give life to children. This gateway should never be opened except in marriage, because when virginity is unlocked, all of a woman's loving response should be allowed to come forth inside a stable relationship. A husband deserves to receive all of his wife's love and she deserves a safe place to give it. Secondly, unlocking virginity also unlocks potential motherhood. Children deserve to come forth in a family built on the covenanted love of a man and a woman who will be father and mother for them."[5]

What about men? God created boundaries for their sexual behavior too. Proverbs 5:9 warns men against engaging in adultery "lest you give your best strength to others and your years to one who is cruel." The passage goes on to warn that if a man scatters his virility, his life will be wasted. We only have to look at all the government programs set up to force recalcitrant fathers to acknowledge their paternity and pay child support, to see the results of men refusing to keep God's rule about chastity and abstinence.

These are the boundaries God established for our sexual behavior. One man and one woman, bound by marriage, producing children. It is impossible to measure the heartbreak, let alone list all the health issues and government programs that have ensued because we chose to operate outside those boundaries.

I came of age in the '60s. That it was an eye-opening experience for me to recognize the truth about God's boundaries for sexuality is a major understatement. I have no choice but to accept the consequences of my own ventures outside those boundaries, and I do. But how much harder it is, how excruciatingly painful it is, to think that I may not be able to spare my precious granddaughters from making the same mistakes.

How, with all the messages and social mores of our culture working against us, will we ever be able to convince the little girls of today that it's not their precious stuffed animal collection or their shoebox full of sparkly costume jewelry that is their greatest treasure to possess, but *their own virtue*—the garden God has given them to protect.

I don't know how we can convince them, I only know we must try. Then maybe some day we will once again be able to go to weddings and witness brides in honest anticipation of giving all they possess, including the secret places of their bodies and souls, to the men who have earned their love and honor by keeping themselves chaste as well. Maybe one of these brides will be your daughter, or my granddaughter. God, make it so.

The Ten Commandments

Another obvious way God created boundaries was when He sent Moses down from the mountain with those immutable Ten Commandments. This was God's first attempt to deliver the truth to us in a way we couldn't miss. Whatever rules you establish as boundaries in your home, they will be sound if they are based on the Ten Commandments.

But when God saw His people were ignoring His boundaries, He knew He had to do more to make His will clear. The inability of the people of Israel to keep God's law pointed to the need for a Savior. They could not meet God's standards on their own and neither can we. That's why God sent Jesus.

Jesus came to earth to close the gap between God and us. He brought with Him a message of grace and forgiveness and showed us how to practice these attributes in our daily lives. He fulfilled the law, but He also brought new commandments: "'Love the Lord your God with all your heart and all your soul and all your mind.' This is the first and greatest commandment. And the second is like it: 'Love your neighbor as yourself'" (Matt. 22:37-39). As He so often did while He walked the earth, Jesus simplified God's intended boundaries for us. If we keep Jesus' commandments, we will be keeping the Ten Commandments as well. And when we accept Him as our Lord and Savior, the Holy Spirit places in our hearts the desire to do so.

The Ten Commandments are found in the Holy Bible, Exodus 20:1-17. Like God's rules for sexual purity, each commandment comes with its own consequences each time the boundary it sets is crossed. Fail to honor your father and mother and there will be conflict within the family. Commit adultery and your marriage will be threatened, if not destroyed.

It is heartening to see average citizens standing up for the right to post the Ten Commandments in public buildings and in schools. So often, it isn't spiritual insight that makes them adamant about passing these rules down to the children they cherish, it's the undeniable truth that keeping these commandments creates boundaries that work, and breaking them creates consequences that cause individuals and society undue grief and expense.

It was encouraging for me to find a contemporary rendition of the Ten Commandments in a secular gift catalog. They were calligraphied in language even the youngest child can understand and printed on a brightly colored plaque. Here are "God's Rules":

> You shall worship no other god but Me.
> You shall not make any statue or picture to worship.
> You shall speak the name of the Lord with reverence.
> You shall keep the Sabbath as a holy day of rest.
> You shall show respect to your father and mother.
> You shall not commit murder.
> You shall be faithful to your husband or wife.
> You shall not steal.
> You shall not speak falsely against others.
> You shall not envy another person's possessions.[6]

Boundaries just don't get any simpler than these, yet it would take volumes to describe all the consequences our society has suffered because we've failed to take God seriously—to believe that He really meant what He said.

In 1999, a Ft. Lauderdale advertising agency launched a nationwide billboard campaign lending a humorous approach to the importance of keeping God's commandments. Each message appeared in white letters against a black background and was signed by God. "What part of 'Thou shalt not' didn't you understand?" read one. "Keep using my name in vain and I'll make rush hour longer" read another. The approach may be humorous, but the truth is undeniable.

Certainly the worst trials and mistakes in my life were a direct result of breaking God's commandments, and I can only assume the same is true for you. Wise parents who want to raise wise kids will begin by explaining God's boundaries to them. Once they understand that there are consequences to moving outside His established boundaries, they will be ready to accept the other necessary boundaries in life. Beginning with the ones established in the home.

Boundaries teach a healthy respect for, and necessary submission to authority. When parents fail to set and enforce boundaries, schools are required to step in and do so. When schools fail, prisons may have to take over.

The book *Boundaries* by Cloud and Townsend spoke to so many people who needed to learn when to say yes and when to say no that it spawned a series of nationwide workshops. I suppose once our society began ignoring God's boundaries, we found it easier to step on one another's toes too. Many obsessive, stressed-out people are being greatly helped by learning to re-establish necessary boundaries in their personal and professional lives. The volume titled *Boundaries with Kids* helps parents apply the principles in *Boundaries* to raising their children to become healthy, well-balanced adults.

The Ten Laws of Boundaries identified by Cloud and Townsend include biblically established guidelines that wise parents incorporate into their lives and pass on to their children. For example, there is the law of sowing and reaping.

"The law of cause and effect is a basic law of life. The Bible calls it the Law of Sowing and Reaping," Cloud and Townsend state. "You reap whatever you sow. If you sow to your own flesh, you will reap corruption from the flesh; but if you sow to the Spirit, you will reap eternal life from the Spirit" (Gal. 6:7-8, NRSV).

"When God tells us that we reap what we sow, he is not punishing us; he's telling us how things really are. If you smoke cigarettes, you most likely will develop a smoker's hack and you may even get lung cancer. If you overspend, you most likely will get calls from creditors, and you may even go hungry because you have no money for food."[7]

Obviously, the examples can go on and on.

And then there is the Law of Respect. Jesus said, "So in everything, do to others what you would have them do to you" (Matt. 7:12).

"We need to respect the boundaries of others. We need to love the boundaries of others in order to command respect for our own. We need to treat their boundaries the way we want them to treat ours," Cloud and Townsend write.[8]

In healthy families, parents learn the importance of boundaries in their own lives first, then they pass this knowledge on to their children. It's not always easy to do. But even children who seem to pull away from the boundaries we have in our homes will eventually return to them, internalize them, and pass them on to their own children.

We can't go wrong if we use the Bible as our guide.

Boundaries in Action

"Train a child in the way he should go, and when he is old he will not turn from it," Proverbs 22:6 instructs us. Deuteronomy 6:6-9 provides more instruction from God through Moses: "These commandments that I give you today are to be upon your hearts.

Impress them on your children. Talk about them when you sit at home and when you walk along the road, when you lie down and when you get up. Tie them as symbols on your hands and bind them on your foreheads. Write them on the doorframes of your houses and on your gates."

In other words, don't wait until your teenager comes home drunk to let him know that isn't a behavior you condone in your household. Don't wait for your daughter to get pregnant to tell her about the boundaries of the secret garden. Rather, as parents, establish healthy ground rules for your home and family and communicate them clearly and often to your children.

And you can't begin too soon. According to Cloud and Townsend, the first boundary of which an infant is aware is the soothing presence of the mother.

"She protects the infant," they write. "Mom's job is to help her newborn contain intense, frightening, and conflicting feelings. Left by themselves, infants are terrorized by their aloneness and lack of internal structure.

"For centuries mothers—including Mary, Jesus' mother—have swaddled their babies or wrapped cloths tightly around them. While swaddling keeps the baby's body heat regulated, the tight wrappings also help the infant feel safe—a sort of external boundary. The baby knows where he or she begins and ends. When newborns are undressed, they often panic about the loss of structure around them."[9]

Older children without boundaries tend to panic too. When parents establish external boundaries, the kids can develop internal ones that both keep them safe and make them feel secure. If such natural boundaries were still in place in our society, maybe we wouldn't need to be talking about artificial ones like metal detectors at the doors of our high schools—and even our elementary schools.

The tragedy at Columbine High School in Littleton, Colorado, on April 20, 1999, shook this state I call home to its very core. How could anything so horrifying be happening on a gorgeous, blue-sky, Colorado spring day?

The lesson this terrible event has to teach us about the importance of boundaries in homes is still unfolding. Amidst all the horror, all the pain, came the story of two parents who took a stand. Their daughter Cassie Bernall died at Columbine that day—not as a perpetrator, as could have been the case, but as an alleged martyr.

Cassie's unquestionable faith in the days and weeks prior to her death consoled a shocked and hurting public. But in the book *She Said Yes, The Unlikely Martyrdom of Cassie Bernall,* by Cassie's mother, Misty Bernall, the rest of the story is told.

Cassie was not always a model teenager, nor was she always a Christian growing up. When she was in her early teens, she became involved with a group of friends who were obsessed with satanic worship and self-mutilation. Her parents found letters in her room that confirmed their daughter and her friends were sniffing glue and, most horrifying of all, were even plotting to kill the Bernalls.

That's when they realized it was time to take action. In an interview given at the time the book was released, Misty Bernall told how she and her husband had tried hard to be Cassie's friends, when what she needed were stronger parents to set boundaries.

"I sometimes feel that with their actions, these kids are crying out for help, and that they will respond positively to someone stepping into their lives and giving them guidance," she said. "I hope parents will understand that it's okay to intervene in your kids' lives and to take a strong stand."[10]

It's okay, but it's not easy. Easier is coaxing, denying, nagging, and becoming totally codependent with a teenager who is acting out: if he has a good day, so do you. If he is in trouble, your day is ruined.

I know because I've been there. One of the key elements to successful boundary tending is consistency. Consistent discipline and enforcement of boundaries is a twenty-four-hour job for the parents of two year olds and teenagers. It's relentless, it's tiring, and it's very difficult for a single mom to do alone.

Things got so out of control with my son Rob during his troubled adolescence that I had to ask him to leave my house. I'm sure many people reading this can't imagine that any mother would ask a seventeen year old to move out on his own, but with the help of the organization Tough Love and intervention from the Lord, I became aware that it was the only answer.

"I can't fix that boy if you won't let him go," I heard God telling me in the dark of night as I cried myself to sleep over Rob one more time. The years of cajoling and rescuing had taken their toll on me, and on my son. He had dropped out of high school three times, been through two drug rehab programs, and had several encounters with the law. It was time to set a boundary: no school, no job, no free room and board with mom.

During Rob's months alone, as he supported himself by frying tortilla chips at a Mexican restaurant, God in His mercy worked a Cassie Bernall-type reformation on my wonderful handsome son. I still remember the day I got the phone call.

"Mom, it's me," I heard my son say. "I want to come home. I miss you, and I miss my family."

I didn't know if he could abide by my rules after living on his own, but he did. Today he is a college graduate, a business owner, a loving husband, and a dad who sets clear, biblically based boundaries for his own two daughters. I can believe that there is great joy in heaven when a prodigal child returns. I've known that joy in my own heart.

I only hope that you will not have to go through the same heartbreak before learning the importance of boundaries in your own home. Children need security. They will keep pushing and pushing until they find a brick wall that won't move. Once they do, they know they are loved.

Children need to feel significant. To know that they matter to their parents and their siblings. To know that they are important contributors to their families. Boundaries in the home show them where they fit into the big picture.

And children need guidance and direction. The kind that comes through clearly communicated discipline and boundaries. "How am I supposed to live?" they are asking as they make their decisions and try to figure out who they are day by precious day.

It takes a home with boundaries to equip children to move out into the world. Gratefully, parents don't have to do this tough job alone. To help them, they have the guidance of God's written Word and the power of His risen Son.

You see, there was another boundary in a garden long ago. It was in a garden where they took the body of the crucified Jesus and laid it in a tomb. A large stone was rolled in front of the tomb, but that was a boundary God would not permit to bind the Son who was to rule with Him for all eternity. Because that stone was rolled away, we have access to all the power in the universe. The Lord who reigns will help you set effective boundaries in your home and give you the strength to enforce them with loving consistency. With Him, all things are possible.

Home Builders:

1. What boundaries do you remember being in place in the home in which you grew up?
2. Are those same boundaries in place in your home today? Why or why not?
3. List more examples of God's natural boundaries. What are the natural consequences that result from living outside of them?

A Home with Integrity

• • • • • • • • • • • • • •

Good, honest, hard-headed character
is the function of the home.

—George A. Dorsey

A friend of mine told a chilling story during a class we were in together at our church. Her mother was an alcoholic and prone to drunken rages. On several occasions the terrified children called the police because they were afraid their mother was going to seriously injure one of them or herself.

But when the police arrived the woman would collect herself sufficiently to persuade the officers there was no problem in that home and that the children were given to pranks. The officers would leave, but as soon as the front door closed the mother would continue her rage with more intensity than before.

Children don't deserve to live in a home that wears one face at the front door and another in the kitchen. My friend just turned forty-five, and she still grieves the childhood she never had.

In a home with integrity, what you see is what you get—all the time. You can drop by a home with integrity without calling ahead because the family living there has nothing to hide. Sure there might be newspapers scattered on the floor on a Sunday afternoon, or dirty dishes in the kitchen sink, but you'll be welcomed anyway. This home is lived in, it's real—and it's honest.

Integrity is most simply defined as honesty. It's an openness that invites inspection. It's an appreciation of those things that have real value, and a turning away from those distractions that would keep us from the best use of our talents, time, and money. In building a home with integrity, we need to begin with the integrity of the people living there. Are they living honest lives and wearing real faces? Is someone protecting the family's time to make sure it's well spent? Is financial integrity being modeled in the disbursement of whatever resources are available for the family to spend, save, or invest?

In a home with integrity, each person living there is clear about who he or she is and what contributions he or she is expected to make for the good of the family and the home. There is no gender or role confusion. Women are allowed to be women, men are allowed to be men, and children are allowed to be children.

In a home with integrity, a man and woman with children to raise are free to be the parents. They make the decisions about what young children will wear, what they will eat, when they will go to bed, and what they will do with their spare time. They talk to their children and endeavor to understand them, yes. But they don't abdicate decision making to them, forcing them to perform adult functions with juvenile minds.

Such parents set and maintain boundaries. They willingly accept this and all other responsibilities of parenting and hold one another accountable.

These same parents give their marriage priority over the wants of the children, making time to be together as a couple, because they know that the marriage is the glue that holds the family together. They model integrity at home and in their work, and would never follow a discussion on the importance of honesty with a request to a child to "tell the paper boy we already paid" if they haven't.

Modeling Integrity

In fact, the very best method for teaching values like integrity to our children is to live them. Two exemplary examples come to mind as I think of this kind of role modeling: a Green Bay Packers star named Reggie White and a low-income single mother named Sonja Carson.

Speaking before the Wisconsin state legislature in March 1998, Reggie White had the courage to speak from his heart on many problems facing our world, including race relations, sexual immorality, greed, obscene movies, and music. He even spoke out about homosexuality. In response to those in the gay rights movement who compare their cause with the black civil rights movement, he stated that the homosexual lifestyle is "a decision . . . not a race." At first the speech was well received, but after an indignant reaction from the media and from gay rights activists, Reggie's honesty cost him corporate sponsorships and a six-million-dollar offer to be a commentator for CBS Sports.

But Reggie White wants to model integrity to his son, Jeremy, and his daughter, Jecolia, so he didn't back away from what he believed in the face of protest. He refused to wear one face at home and another in front of the microphones.

"I'm not going to sell out," he said. "I'm not going to back off what I know God has put on my heart to share. God owns a whole lot more than CBS could ever give me."[1]

The stand Sonja Carson took in the lives of her boys was equally firm, but also so wise and tender that I'm moved to tears whenever I consider her story. She too modeled integrity in the way she lived her life—even to the extent of being open and honest about her own shortcomings.

"Every mom knows that a child isn't going to hear too much of what she says," Sonya Carson said. "It's what she does that is important. You have to start living what you say."

Determined to save her sons from the violence in the streets that claims so many young black men, Sonya Carson determined that her sons, Curtis and Ben, would do their homework as soon as they got home from school. She limited their TV watching to two programs a week, and told them the rest of their free time was to be spent reading. In the meantime, she took whatever job she could find to keep them fed and housed.

"Both of my boys could read much better than I could," Sonja said. "So I had them read me my favorite book—the book of Proverbs. Then I asked them to explain to me what they had read."

The boys did as their mother said, but as they became more educated, they became embarrassed by her lack of formal education. "Teach me. If you can't teach me, don't criticize me," was her humble response.[2]

Because of Sonja Carson's model of integrity and perseverance, her sons did far more than reach adulthood. Curtis Carson went to the University of Michigan and today is an accomplished engineer. Ben went to Yale for his undergraduate degree, then on to the University of Michigan for his M.D.—all on scholarships. Today, Ben is the director of pediatric neurosurgery at Johns Hopkins Hospital and one of the world's most renowned surgeons. These men are who they are today because Sonja Carson knew her role as a parent, and lived up to it.

When parents act like parents, then children can be children. The popular pizza parlor Chuck E. Cheese invites families to come for pizza and a show "where a kid can be a kid."™ How sad it is if we live in a society where kids can no longer be kids in their own homes.

Why can't they? For some, it may be because they are latchkey children and have to be the adults-in-residence—they're in charge. If they're children in single-parent families, they may have to shoulder at least some of the responsibilities and chores of the missing parent. Even children in two-parent families may be so over-scheduled with sports activities, enrichment opportunities, and music lessons that they have no time left to "be a kid."

Integrity in How We Spend Our Time

Isn't it ironic that the same parents who fondly recall going barefoot in the summer and lying on their backs creating imaginary shapes in the clouds—the ones who drank bottles of orange pop and put the bottle caps in the spokes of their bicycles—are lining up in droves to sign their kids up for competitive sports and accelerated academics programs.

Today's kids are adding daily planners to the load of school books in their backpacks, the average weight of which has doctors alarmed about the misalignment of growing spines. They carry cell phones and pagers instead of yo-yos. Backyard circuses and lemonade stands are endangered at best. It's hard to be a kid in such a world.

In a home with integrity, the wise use of time is consistently evaluated. God has allotted each one of us a certain number of days, but no one knows how much time he has left. Like the psalmist, we can only ask that He would "teach us to number our days aright, that we may gain a heart of wisdom" (Ps. 90:12).

The families of students who have died in school shootings or bus accidents didn't know that their time together would abruptly and violently end when they sent their kids out the door that morning. We don't know how much time we have with our kids. We only know that time is a precious gift from God—one He allows us to monitor and spend as we choose.

In a home with integrity, parents support their children in the activities in which they really want to get involved, but don't push them into areas where they have neither the aptitude nor the desire to participate. The fact that the neighbors' children have signed up isn't a good enough reason for their kids to do the same. Rather, they take the time to get to know their children well before suggesting or supporting their participation in any activity that will impact the family schedule.

When this sort of discretion isn't used, children can become just as stressed as the most over-booked adults.

Columnist Kathleen Parker was alarmed to read that only 25 percent of the American child's day is unstructured. Whereas she recalls kids in the '50s spending more than half their time engaged in imaginative unstructured activities like sand-lot kickball or weaving clover chains, today's kids rarely even have recess at school. Instead, they have "organized fun."

"When we deprive children of play, after all, we're depriving them of innocence," Parker writes. "In the past twenty years, we've so blurred the lines between adults and children that their language, schedules and activities mirror our own."[3]

So does their stress level.

Research shows that one in three children suffers from chronic stress symptoms and that children as young as three suffer from stress-related illnesses like ulcerative colitis. One in twenty children under age ten suffers from depression, a typical stress-related condition, and suicide is now the third most common form of death among teens.[4]

Where can kids go to be kids? Hopefully, they can go home, to parents who will protect them from too many activities too soon, and who will make unstructured playtime for everybody in the family, especially the children, a top priority.

According to Barbara Mahany of the *Chicago Tribune*, "The notion of the over-scheduled child is not new. What's unsettling is that for so many kids it's the way life is, and it's coming at them younger and more furiously all the time."[5]

David Elkind was among the first to draw attention to the

problem of the loss of childhood in our country when he released his best-selling book *The Hurried Child: Growing Up Too Fast Too Soon* in 1981. When he revised the book in 1988, he reported the problem wasn't getting better. Interviewed in 1999, Elkind said, "I've been around to lots of affluent communities recently. Status used to be the car you drove, the clothes you wore. Now everybody drives fancy cars, wears fancy clothes. That's not the issue anymore. Now it's 'Where's your kid; what's your kid doing?' Children have become our main symbols of conspicuous consumption."[6]

In communities where "affluenza" is rampant, a stay-at-home mom is more than likely a stay-in-the-car mom as she spends every afternoon getting her kids to their lessons and practices. Could it be that the competition among high-achieving parents has actually made it more fun to be in a family with fewer resources where children are allowed to stay home a few afternoons a week?

Making decisions about how much activity is too much activity is a parent's responsibility, not a child's. In a home with integrity, a parent doesn't hesitate to step in and take control of the family's schedule. I believe we owe it to our children to help them say no to many of the opportunities they have to be over scheduled. We'll know we made the right choice when we see a look of relief come over their faces as they run outside to play.

It saddened me to see a public service announcement on television encouraging parents to consider having a meal together with the whole family around the kitchen table at the same time. Are family dinners so rare that they have to be promoted on television? Other spots encourage parents to read to their young children. In a home with integrity, these things happen every day as a matter of course and are part of the daily rhythm of the family—not uniquely scheduled events. If a family is too busy to have dinner together at least three times a week, they're too busy. If parents are never available to read to their children, then quite frankly, their priorities are out of order.

Not only must we begin reading to our children again, but we need to consider what we read. Our choices can profoundly affect the development of virtues like integrity and responsibility.

In the introduction to *The Book of Virtues,* William J. Bennett, the former Secretary of Education during the Reagan administration, explains why he felt it was imperative to pull together a collection of classic literature for today's families. The stories, he said, "give children some specific reference points. Our literature and history are a rich quarry of moral literacy. We should mine that quarry. Children must have at their disposal a stock of examples illustrating what we see to be right and wrong, good and bad—examples illustrating that, in many instances, what is morally right and wrong can indeed be known and promoted."[7]

Most of us learned about kindness from stories like "The Mouse and the Lion." We learned about perseverance from "The Tortoise and the Hare." We learned that honesty never goes out of fashion by reading "The Emperor's New Clothes." Sadly, many teachers and parents have forgotten the moral value of reading such stories to children, not to mention the Bible stories about Daniel in the lion's den or David defeating Goliath with his slingshot. Reading provides parents with a wonderful opportunity to teach without teaching.

So does conversation. In an age when we are constantly checking in with voice mail systems and e-mail sites, parents need to resist the temptation to get a jump on the day by calling in to their office voice mail while driving children to school. After all, it's during those precious few minutes in the car that they can tune in to the ups and downs their kids are experiencing, answer questions, both spoken and unspoken, and confirm family plans for the evening.

In a home with integrity and an understanding of the value of time, conversation is valued over almost any other activity. Astute parents realize that quality conversations happen spontaneously far more often than they can be planned. They also know that a question like "What was the best thing and the worst thing that happened to you today?" will get a better response from a child than "How was school?"

Some of the best conversations I ever had with my grandmother took place on the back porch of our house in Tennessee. There she would sit with the big aluminum bowl in her lap as she methodically snapped the string beans. I would help with the beans, but the whole time I would be thinking of what I wanted to ask Granny next. We would both be lulled by the snap, snap, snap of the string bean symphony. Then I would ask a question, knowing it could be quite a few more snaps before I got an answer. My questions were both trivial and monumental, but the answers always seemed profound.

Sociologists believe that the mother-daughter relationship was damaged by the invention of the dishwasher. In pre-dishwasher homes (for those of you too young to remember), Mom washed the dishes while her daughter stood by her side drying them. With the dishtowel and saucer in her hand, looking out the kitchen window instead of at her mother, it was easier for a twelve-year-old girl to ask the burning questions inside her. Questions like, "How did you know you were really in love?" or "Does it hurt to have a baby?"

Likewise, many men recall the conversations they had with their dads out in the driveway working on the family Buick. Chances are the two of them had their most significant exchanges between "pass me the wrench" and "OK, give it some gas." Somehow it's easier to talk about touchy subjects like the "birds and bees" when you're busy working at the same time.

And those important conversations need to take place much earlier than they did with our parents. According to the results of a study conducted by the Kaiser Family Foundation and Children

Now, two groups that co-sponsor the Talking With Kids About
Tough Issues campaign, children aren't getting all the information
they want early enough.

Among the ten-to-twelve year olds surveyed, 50 percent said
they wanted more information about both how to protect against
HIV/AIDS and what to do if someone brings a gun to school; 44
percent wanted to know more about how to handle pressure to
have sex; and 43 percent wanted more discussion of how to know
if they're ready to have sex, and how drugs and alcohol might
influence their decisions.[8]

Clearly, if we aren't talking to our kids about these issues,
someone else will. Isn't it better for them to hear our perspective
first? Before they hear the messages of relativity and compromise,
shouldn't they hear that the Bible says there is a difference
between right and wrong, and that choices have consequences?

Some of the mistakes we make in parenting seem almost
irreversible. The toddler without boundaries becomes the
teenager who breaks curfew. We reap what we sow. The good
news is that it's never too late to make conversation a part of our
family life together. Still, it's easier to talk about major, life-changing topics with preteens if we've established the habit of family
conversation when they were younger.

Since 1920, the Child Welfare League of America (CWLA) has
been developing and promoting policies and programs to nurture, strengthen, and protect America's children and families.

"When families regularly sit down together for a meal, children have a comfortable routine to enhance their communication
skills," says Karabelle Pizzigati, Ph.D., of the CWLA. "Healthy family conversation at mealtime builds a child's self-confidence and
positive family interaction, providing parents with a window into
the child's world."[9]

A brochure published by CWLA listed these ideas for encouraging mealtime conversation:

- **Roundtable Stories:** Construct a story with one family member contributing a sentence and the next family member building from it.
- **"What would you do?":** Challenge the family with tricky situations and moral dilemmas, varying the situations depending on age. (In Christian families, this could be changed to "What would Jesus do?")
- **Brain teasers:** Take turns asking "brain teaser" questions or riddles.
- **Geography:** Serve dinner items from a particular region of the world, such as China or Mexico, and talk about that country.[10]

Once you get people comfortable talking again, and the vows of silence have been broken, it will be easier to stimulate conversation by inviting children to tell narratives and stories, or give descriptions of people they know or places they've been. When parents talk about their day in terms children can understand, the conversation provides valuable insight into what it means to be a man or a woman—an adult in the real world.

Obviously, a home with conversation in it is a home with less of other activities—especially television. It's a home where time is considered too precious to be wasted watching TV programs we don't really want to watch or surfing Internet sites out of sheer boredom.

"Whatever is true, whatever is noble, whatever is right, whatever is pure, whatever is lovely, whatever is admirable—if anything is excellent or praiseworthy—think about such things," Paul advised in Philippians 4:8. I often think that if we all had that verse posted above our TVs, our watching time would be drastically reduced. With a few programming exceptions, TV is a waste of our family's precious time together.

An article in *World Magazine* previewing the television offerings for fall '99 summarized the concerns about most programming this way: "Language once regarded as taboo . . . is now the common parlance of the TV world. Sitcoms once content with sexual innuendoes now make explicit sex jokes. Dramas once sprinkled with fistfights and bloodless shootouts now revel in showing rotting corpses and people burning alive."[11]

My husband and I love it when the grandkids sleep over and we have an excuse to start our day with "Sesame Street." Whether it's "Monsterpiece Theater" with Alistair Cookie Monster, or Miss Piggy singing, "I'm just a cereal girl," we always enjoy the adult humor interspersed with the attention-getting educational content aimed at the kids. But now even public television, including children's programming, is coming under fire as being positioned so far to the political left that many question whether it still merits being publicly funded. It's the lesser of two evils, but still not good in excess.

"Television is a seductive monster that is swallowing more and more of the most valuable commodity in life—time," columnist Mona Charen wrote. "In 1960, the average American watched five hours of television per day. Today, he watches seven hours. Teenagers watch about twenty-one hours per week, in contrast to 5.6 hours spent doing homework, 1.8 hours reading and thirty-five minutes talking with their fathers.

"It isn't just the content of TV, it's the passivity of television watching that should alarm us," she continued. "Television is mind Novocaine. It lulls and dulls the faculties. And there is what economists call the 'opportunity cost.' Time spent in front of the box is time not spent discovering, playing, reading, inventing, imagining and interacting."[12]

In the interest of redeeming her family's time, Charen was tempted to put her family TV sets in the attic, but was convinced by a friend that limiting TV watching to weekends would prevent the "forbidden fruit" syndrome in her young children.

"What amazes me is how easy it is to relinquish TV," she writes. "Television was omnipresent in our lives, but its absence is noted almost entirely in positive terms. It's like finding that a blanket you thought was keeping you warm was actually making it hard to breathe."[13]

Other parents have made other choices.

"When the children started memorizing the commercials, begging for toys of which I had never heard, and lying around mesmerized for hours, it seemed like a good time to take the plunge into a TV-free environment. So we unplugged the set," wrote Robin Zenger Baker, a young mother of three children, ages eight, seven, and three. "As one might guess, our lifestyle had to adjust to accommodate the death of its most entertaining member. I'll admit I worried that I wouldn't be able to get anything done without my built-in baby-sitter. Yet what happened was a pleasant surprise."[14]

Robin goes on to describe the creativity she began to see come alive in her children, and the positive aspects of spending more quality time with them because of turning off the TV.

When it comes to TV watching, it may not be necessary to throw out the baby with the bath water, but homes with integrity protect precious time by monitoring the hours and programs children are allowed to watch. They also monitor their children's computer time and access to the Internet, limiting the sites they are allowed to visit.

When our granddaughter Amanda was two, she had an amazing knack for forming two-word sentences that completely expressed whatever she wanted to say or ask. After watching a video downstairs with her sister, she came upstairs to tell my husband, "Movie over." One day she approached me in the kitchen with a simple request, "Play 'puter?" Imagine my surprise when I put her on a pillow in my office chair and watched her begin to manipulate and click the mouse adroitly as she moved through an interactive storybook.

We cannot deny that our children will spend much of their lifetimes on the computer, but we can put the family computer in a room where it can be easily monitored or take advantage of monitoring devices available. Whatever it takes, responsible parents will monitor computer use with the same vigilance with which they monitor their children's choice of TV programs, videos, music, and movies. Even the positive uses of computers can become problematic if children are spending too much time in front of the screen in lieu of a variety of productive activities.

Financial Integrity

Parents in homes with integrity also clearly think through and communicate to their children the position and power that money will be given in their family. Then, of course, they model financial integrity themselves.

It does no good to tell your daughter that family is your top priority if you are so busy making money that you only make one out of five of her soccer games. Children believe what they experience. They overhear the arguments and discussions that can occur in any household when it's time to pay the bills. They also notice when dad gets a new car because the neighbors got one, or when mom comes home with a new wardrobe every season.

To the extent that it is our quest for perfection that often fuels our desire to do and have more, Dr. Craig Barnes, senior pastor of The National Presbyterian Church in Washington, D.C., suggests that we need to consider embracing the idea that enough may very well be enough.

"I think it is high time the church introduces the concept of 'good enough,'" he writes in his book *Hustling God.* "You are not the perfect worker. You are not the perfect mom or dad or child. But you are probably good enough. You do not have the perfect home, the perfect job, or the perfect body. But it is probably good enough. Life comes with scratches and cracks. That can either preoccupy you with improvement plans, or it can be the opportunity to give thanks to God who insists on loving us only by grace. . . . There is so much freedom waiting for anyone who would settle for good enough. It will free you to turn your attention to the perfect work of your Savior."[15]

The concept of "good enough" certainly applies to our desire to acquire, too. How easy it is to get caught up in the advertisements for the latest model car, the most innovative kitchen appliance, the tiniest cell phone, or the newest line of designer clothing. If your children are asking for shoes and shirts by brand name, it may be time to do a better job of modeling what really matters in terms of material possessions. If you can honestly communicate that enough is enough, and demonstrate that you are not driven by a desire to acquire, just maybe you have a chance of combating the strong messages dumped on them by advertisers and peers.

It won't be easy.

A significant number of Americans are living in enormous houses they can't afford to furnish and driving cars they can't afford to fill with gas, all with the goal of keeping up a certain image. As one of our pastors puts it, they are "spending money they don't have to buy things they don't need in order to impress people they don't know." Parents in such homes often compensate for not having enough time for their children by buying them more and more stuff. Each year, Americans spend an estimated twenty-four billion dollars on their children for everything from the latest fads to high-tech electronic devices. It isn't necessarily wrong to spend money on our kids, but it's wrong if we're spending money instead of time. And it's wrong if our spending fails to reflect financial integrity.

Curiously, authentically wealthy people are not big spenders who flaunt their bank accounts and stock portfolios, but quietly comfortable millionaires who teach their children the value of money. They hold to the principle that the key to financial security is to earn more than they spend—and do it for a long time.

Researchers Thomas J. Stanley and William D. Danko, authors

of the best-selling book *The Millionaire Next Door,* proved that following old principles is still the best way to accumulate wealth. After studying the spending and saving habits of wealthy Americans, they found these were people who are efficient with their time and money, who "believe that financial independence is more important than displaying high social status," and who "live well below their means."[16]

When I asked Tom Stanley his perception of how these discreet millionaires communicate their financial integrity to their children, he said they model their values every day at the kitchen table.

"It may surprise you to hear that most millionaires do their own grocery shopping. They make grocery lists, not only because they don't want to buy something they don't need, but because they don't won't to waste thirty minutes in the grocery store," Stanley said. "They live in households that are productive in that they have schedules and budgets and they follow both. Children see this modeled day in and day out."

It won't be easy to create a home with financial integrity when your children are exposed to so much financial disparity in our society. They know the salaries of professional athletes, and they see the used cars their teachers drive to work. Everywhere they hear the message that more is better, and most of them believe anything can be purchased with a credit card or a trip to the ATM.

As in all aspects we've discussed for creating a God-ordained home, His Word is the best place to turn for instruction on teaching your children financial integrity. Discuss Proverbs 6:8 about the industrious ant. Talk about what Jesus meant when He said, "Do not store up for yourselves treasures on earth" in Matthew 6 and "a man's life does not consist in the abundance of his possessions" in Luke 12.

"You cannot serve both God and Money," Jesus said in Luke 16. Explain to your children why this is true. Make them aware of the ways your family gives to help others, and encourage them to do the same with the allowances they earn. Help them understand that all our resources belong to God anyway. When we give, we are merely returning to Him what is already His.

Whether we're talking about integrity of roles, time, finances, or other resources, the best instruction technique is still modeling the integrity you want your children to have. Be home when you say you will be home. Deal honestly with neighbors and service people. Establish guidelines for resourceful uses of time and money, and keep them yourself.

You may also have to swallow your pride in order to model integrity. Admitting when we are wrong, and apologizing to our children, shows them that even the best parents are fallible. When we really mess up, our kids know it. It is recorded in Luke 10:21 that Jesus once said, "I praise you, Father, Lord of heaven and earth, because you have hidden these things from the wise and learned, and revealed them to little children." Children have a God-given wisdom we can only begin to understand. They know when we have done something wrong. Asking for their forgiveness not only heals the hurt, it teaches them integrity in dealing with their own shortcomings.

Do you know where the checkerboard is? How long has it been since you played a rousing game of Monopoly or Go Fish? It's not too late to spend fun, imaginative times with your children. Even if they have already flown the nest, play games at your next holiday get-together. It will reveal a great deal about how your young adults are coping with life. Make time to play and talk—not just for the fun of it, but because spending time with your children is the very best way to teach integrity.

"Today we speak about values and how it is important to 'have them,' as if they were beads on a string or marbles in a pouch," William Bennett writes in the introduction to his collection of classic tales. "But these stories speak to morality and virtues not as something to have but as something to be, the most important thing to be."[17]

Character does count, and the best opportunity children will have to develop it is to grow up in a home with integrity.

♡ Home Builders:

1. When we are honest before God, our children will see a picture of integrity. What are some ways you model integrity in your own life?
2. It's said that the quickest way to find out what we value most is to look in our checkbooks. Where does your money go? What would your checkbook tell your kids you value most?
3. Using time wisely is a virtue, but it's wrong to have every minute of every day so tightly scheduled that families are always "doing" at the expense of "being." What are some activities you could afford to eliminate from your family calendar?

A Home with Hope

. . . .

Hope, child, tomorrow and tomorrow still,
and every tomorrow hope; trust while you live.
Hope, each time the dawn doth heaven fill,
be there to ask as God is there to give.

—*Victor Hugo*

Of all the legacies parents can leave their children, none is more valuable than the legacy of hope based on a belief in Jesus Christ as Lord and Savior. Family heirlooms may be lost or stolen, houses and businesses will eventually crumble, but this legacy of hope can be safely handed down from generation to generation of those who love the Lord.

Children have many little troubles in the course of a normal day. Someone is mean to them on the playground. They forget their jackets. The teacher yells at them. They mourn when the gerbil dies or the family cat gets run over by a car. But increasingly, truly monumental sorrows are visiting the hearts and minds of America's children.

We just can't send our children out of our homes without filling their hearts with hope. The world can be far too painful for adults, let alone kids. An accident that happened just a few miles from our home was so chilling that I still think of it every time I pass by the scene. A mother and her friend were taking their pre-school sons to the state fair for a day of rides, cotton candy, and maybe a few too many hot dogs.

A truck driver remembers seeing the two little boys strapped into their seat belts in the backseat of the car laughing and motioning to him to blow his horn when their vehicle passed his. A few moments later, the same driver was fighting back flames in a desperate attempt to get the little boys out of the car. One boy was pulled out, although his burns were so severe he will always be disabled and scarred. The other, only four years old, perished in the flames.

No one knows exactly why the four-wheel-drive vehicle swerved out of control, bounced off a guardrail, and flipped onto its roof. No one knows why the accident made the car burst into flames. In the end, why doesn't matter. The mom who was driving lost her son; her friend's son is horribly damaged both emotionally and physically.

Another family we know was devastated to learn that their nine-year-old daughter, the third of four girls in the family, had an inoperable brain tumor. Frantically, they tried one treatment after the next. Days were spent making long trips to a large hos-pital in a neighboring city, and nights were spent researching the disease on the Internet in hopes of finding a miracle cure. But in spite of all their love and care, the little girl died.

These are just two of the tragedies I think of when I think of people being put in the position of bearing the unbearable. You could come up with your own examples, I'm sure. I can't imagine how hard it must be to survive such horrendous losses. If you sleep at all after something like this happens, how do you deal with the reality of it when you wake up the next morning? What do you do first? What do you say?

In her book, *Harsh Grief, Gentle Hope,* Mary White writes of the agony she and her husband suffered after their son Stephen was killed in a random shooting while driving his cab late one night. She gives an account of her first thoughts, and it is heartbreaking to read of her struggle to accept this truth too horrible to comprehend.[1]

But what helped the Whites cope with Stephen's death is that they created and lived in a home with hope. Doing the same will help prepare our families for similar tragedies if they happen. The grief we feel when someone we love dies will still wash over us in painful waves, yes, but we will not have to "grieve like the rest of men, who have no hope" (1 Thess. 4:13).

A home with hope is a home where the reality of the risen Lord is a part of daily life. It's a home steeped in the comfort and healing of the promise of eternal life through belief in Jesus Christ. It is a home where those inside are living out stories with happy endings written long ago by the hand of God.

Remember the little sixteen-month-old girl, Anna, who died after a two-week battle with E. coli bacteria due to drinking bottled apple juice? I wondered if the parents were Christian when I heard on the news that they had decided not to sue the juice manufacturer. Later an Associated Press wire story confirmed my suspicions when it reported the family said they would "rely on their Christian faith to carry on."

As so often happens when the media focuses on one family's tragedy, little Anna's parents were thrust into the national spotlight. How did God use what happened for good? He gave them the courage to share their faith with the nation.

"We don't blame the [juice] company at all," Anna's mother said. "They had no bad intentions throughout all of this."

"We can't understand everything that happens in this world," the little girl's father told reporters through his tears. "I wanted Anna to grow up and do something to serve God—to help people touch God in some way. I think she's already done that."[2]

Obviously, those are parents who rely on a hope greater than any earthly hope we know—hope they had no doubt already begun to instill in little Anna before she died. That's what parents do when they build homes with hope.

When Children Lead the Way

Yet sometimes the roles reverse, and it is the children who lead the parents back into a deeper faith. A common pattern even among young adults who went to church as children is to forget about going to church once they are out on their own or first married. While their faith may survive, their affiliation with a church may not. But when children are born, the parents are more likely to activate their faith and return to church holding the hands of little boys in clip-on ties and little girls in patent leather shoes.

The faith that brings them back to the church is the same faith that will fill their homes with hope. We read in Hebrews 10:23-25, "Let us hold unswervingly to the hope we profess, for he who promised is faithful. And let us consider how we may spur one another on toward love and good deeds. Let us not give up meeting together, as some are in the habit of doing, but let us encourage one another."

Children leading their parents back to church are fulfilling part of the promise Jesus saw in them when he said, "Let the little children come to me, and do not hinder them, for the kingdom of heaven belongs to such as these" (Matt. 19:14).

Certainly, the honesty and simplicity with which children approach the throne fills all our hearts with hope—and provides more than a few tears and chuckles along the way.

"Children know the grace of God better than most of us," Archibald MacLeish wrote. "They see the world the way the morning brings it back to them, new and born and fresh and wonderful."

It's always amusing when children get the stories they hear in Sunday School just a bit wrong. Like the little boy who came home from church and told his parents that Jesus had a cross-eyed teddy bear named Gladly. "How did you ever get that idea?" the parents asked. "We sang a song about him," the little boy replied. "Gladly, the cross I bear."

A four-year-old girl we know helped her mom unpack the "Jesus kit" she had requested they add to the family Christmas decorations. "Oh, here's Mary!" she exclaimed. "Here's Jesus. This must be Joseph. And here are the holy goats!"

Churches go back and forth about whether to say "trespasses" or "debts" in the Lord's Prayer, but one five-year-old theologian straightened it all out when he prayed, "Forgive us our trash baskets as we forgive those who put trash in our baskets." Any preacher worth his salt could turn that one statement into a six-week series on forgiveness.

And yet these same children, who come to God's Word so fresh and eager to learn, can become embittered adults. If they go to church but come home to parents who have not created a home filled with hope all week long, they may decide the faith they hear about at church is not real. They become resigned to believing that this world is all there is, and they join the population who just go to church for Easter, Christmas, and the occasional funeral.

I can't imagine living without hope in a life eternal. And I certainly can't imagine facing minor illness and disappointment, let alone major tragedy, without it. As long as we live we will be faced with situations that test our faith. But when we are living in homes with hope, and have the hope that exceeds understanding in our hearts, we will be ready for the test.

An Anchor for the Soul

One of the most joyous occasions I've hosted in our home in many years was a bridal shower for a good friend who was getting married for the first time at forty-one. After years of believing she would probably be single for the rest of her life, she met a strong Christian man of fifty-four and fell head over heels in love.

The two of them were married just six weeks when her cherished husband wrecked on his bike. He was thrown over the handlebars onto the trail with such force that he suffered spinal cord damage, and months later he is still paralyzed from the chest down. In the face of such disappointment and heartache, not to mention concern about her husband's long-term health, my friend Dana was sustained by her faith.

"It is only in the hope I have in Christ that I can endure this sorrow," she wrote in her e-mail message to a group of friends who had been praying for her and her husband. "His strength exceeds my adequacy and my ability to cope."

Daily as Dana sat by Rich's bed in the hospital, she searched the Scripture for promises of God in which the two of them could trust. "Those who hope in the Lord will renew their strength," she read again and again. "They will soar on wings like eagles; they will run and not grow weary, they will walk and not be faint" (Isa. 40:31).

I used to like the motto stitched on pillows and printed on bumper stickers that said, "God couldn't be everywhere, that's why He created mothers." Now I realize that God can be everywhere, He just chooses to use mothers and fathers to instill His children with messages of hope so that when bad things happen, they will have the only faith that can sustain them through it. Dana grew up with a mom who is a staunch prayer warrior in spite of her own health problems, and a dad who shares his wife's faith. Had she not grown up in a home with hope, it's likely she never could have survived her husband's accident, let alone what she would face next.

The day before Rich was to be released from the rehabilitation hospital, Dana was on her way to sign the lease on the handicap-accessible apartment they found when she was involved in an inexplicable head-on collision. Officers investigating the accident can only surmise that someone may have clipped her rear bumper, causing her car to swerve out of control, roll across the median, and slam into a minivan headed in the other direction.

Within minutes, she was rushed to the emergency room in the hospital adjacent to her husband's where she had to lay on a suspended, swinging board for two days until the swelling in her spine went down. Then the doctors performed a nine-hour surgery on her back. Gratefully, the surgery was a success and she can walk again, but she faces a long, slow recovery.

My own faith was temporarily shaken the day I heard about the wreck. "God, what can You be thinking?" I yelled at the top of my lungs. As I prayed, God kept reassuring me that everything would be okay, and that He intended to use even this new tragedy for good. When I went to see Dana, she wasn't the least bit bitter about what had happened to her. "It's only by the grace of God that I'm alive, and that I can walk," she kept saying. "Only by the grace of God." Clearly, there will be more to the story of Dana and Rich. Whether he regains complete use of his limbs or not, God will make something good come out of their faithfulness, and they will be together in a home with hope—on earth and in heaven.

I've come to understand that the question we need to ask in times of trial like this is not, "Why me?" but rather, "Why not me?"

"In this world you will have trouble," Jesus promised. "But take heart! I have overcome the world" (John 16:33). Because we are residents of a fallen world, left here by a God who loved us enough to give us the gift of free will, accidents happen, disease takes hold, and tragedy awaits.

But God sent His Son so that in spite of what happens to us, we will have "this hope as an anchor for the soul, firm and secure" (Heb. 6:19). He doesn't promise to insulate us from pain, but to be with us in the midst of it. He will deliver us from it or through it, but He will deliver us. We have this hope because Jesus is alive. This is a concept so profound scholars could write volumes about it, but so simple, the smallest child can grasp it and treasure it in her heart. We owe it to our precious children to send them out in the world equipped with this hope.

When my granddaughter Amanda was three I suspected that she might have a hearing disability because everything she said was yelled at the top of her lungs. Finally we decided she wasn't hard of hearing. She just wanted to make sure she was heard over the chatter of her five-year-old sister and the adult conversations around her.

One Easter Sunday we were driving home from church, and I was snuggled into the middle seat belt in the backseat because both of the girls wanted to sit next to Grancy. (You won't believe the things you'll do for your grandchildren until you have them!)

All of a sudden Amanda excitedly announced so loudly that she startled everyone in the car: JESUS ISN'T DEAD ANYMORE! We laughed in surprise, but I wipe a tear or two now every time I think of that day. This little three year old had been paying attention in Sunday School, and the seed of hope had been planted in her heart. It's a hope that will continue to grow, eventually creating a windbreak to help her withstand whatever storms will lash at her in her lifetime.

Our church calls its Sunday School for kids Promiseland, based on the promises of God that the teachers pray they will be able to instill in the hearts of children. Certainly it lived up to its name in the heart and mind of one little visitor that Easter morning.

Can a home with hope exist even if the family does not go to church? It can. It's possible to have family devotions at campsites and on hikes in the woods. It's possible to share faith every day in little ways: a grace at meal, bedtime prayers, even the occasional Scripture verse on the refrigerator door.

But families who truly want to create a home with hope realize the importance of coming together in the fellowship of believers where they can learn from and lean on one another. When children see their parents wanting to go to church to grow in their faith and nurture the hope in their hearts, they understand that worship is not just an exercise for children, but a life-long process for everyone. Going to church on Sunday equips the whole family for living a Christ-filled life all week long. Likewise, there are many things that can be done in the home to reinforce and model what is learned at church.

When this book was just past the proposal stage, I went to a women's retreat in the sleepy little town of Waxahachie, Texas. Several of the conferees and I were having lunch in the local diner when someone asked me if I was working on a new book. I said I was, and I began talking about the concept for *It Takes a Home*. I shared my vision that it would encourage parents to realize the power they have, in God, to create homes that honor Him. Then I listed the chapters I was planning: A Home with a Mom, A Home with a Dad, A Home with Hope and so on.

After lunch, the group decided to browse together through an antique store next door to the diner. I was looking at a statue of a cat with green marble eyes when one of the other women ran up excitedly and handed me a book she had found in the used book pile.

The book was *The Home Beautiful* by J. R. Miller, written in 1912. Imagine my surprise when I turned to the table of contents and saw chapters on mothers, fathers, and faith in the home. Needless to say, I felt it was well worth the four-dollar price tag, so I bought it.

One of the things I love best about old books, and I've collected quite a few, is to read the inscriptions in the front. I love wondering about the giver and the recipient. Who were they? And what were the circumstances in which the book was given?

In this case the mystery was fairly easy to solve because the inscription reads, "Wishing you two much happiness." It was a wedding gift, given in the hope that some young couple would begin to build a home with hope. In the chapter titled, "Religion in the Home," the author wrote:

> Every home in the world is exposed to a thousand dangers. Enemies seek to destroy it, to desecrate its holy beauty and to carry away its sacred treasures. The very institution itself is assailed by the apostles of infidelity and licentiousness. Countless social influences tend to disintegrate the home, to rob it of its sanctities, to break down its sacred barriers and to sully its purity. Nothing but the cross of Christ will save it. Those who are setting up a home, their hearts full of precious hopes of happiness and blessing, should consecrate it at once by erecting the altar of God in the midst of it.[3]

Everything changes, yet everything remains the same. Except for the language sounding a bit more erudite than the English most writers use today, Miller could as easily be writing about a home in the twenty-first century as one in 1912. The altar he suggests is not a physical one, of course, but rather the attitude and willingness of our hearts to make God—His Word, His commandments, His love—the center of our home life.

Spiritual Disciplines

How do we do this? One way is to consciously model to our children the spiritual disciplines that draw us closer to Jesus Christ. Disciplines like: meditation, prayer, worship, solitude, study, confession, service, and even fasting—if not from food, then from television or other activities that prevent God from being the family altar.

Children may first be aware of their parents observing a spiritual discipline when they see their parents studying or having "quiet time." In a book she is writing on the subject, Carla Williams describes the ways she and her husband modeled this and other spiritual disciplines to their children. She writes, "One day I awoke to find six-year-old Joshua missing from his bed. Concerned, I searched the quiet, dark house for him. I found my son kneeling in the living room praying with his Bible opened before him. When Joshua noticed me, he ran over and gave me a big hug. With a smile as bright as the sun dawning in the window he said, 'Good morning, Mom! I set my alarm for 6:00 so I could get a quiet time alone with God.'"[4]

Carla and her husband also established the practice of having a daily devotion, worship, and prayer time with their children in the morning before school. They believed that sending them out the door with God on their minds was the best defense they could give their children against whatever the world would send their way that day. Again, her children noticed.

"When our youngest son Josiah was in kindergarten," Carla writes, "we left the house for school one day in a hurry. As a result, we had not had our daily quiet time of prayer and worship. On the way to school Josiah spoke up, 'Mommy, I think we forgot to take Jesus with us.'"[5]

A home with hope takes the time to develop spiritual disciplines in the children who reside there, the same children who leave their peanut butter sandwich crusts under the bed and track mud through the living room. These little people will never be perfect any more than their parents will, but they can go out into the world armed with the armor of God.

In Ephesians 6 this armor is described as the belt of truth, the breastplate of righteousness, the gospel of peace, the shield of faith, the helmet of salvation, and the sword of the Spirit, which is the Word of God. I often wonder if we spend too much time making sure our children have their mittens and hats, their lunchboxes and their permission slips, and too little time giving them the things they really need each time they leave the house.

Susan Miller is a mom who knows how important it is to equip children sufficiently for the battles of each day. "When I drop my children off at school in the morning, I make the sign of the cross on their foreheads and give them a blessing such as: 'Go with God, serve Him well,' or 'Remember, you belong to God,'" she said. "I do this because as I am sending them into the world for the day—and heading to work myself—I want them to remember their true center point. Recently, my son has been reciprocating the action by giving me the sign of the cross and speaking a blessing to me!"[6]

Our children desperately need our blessings and our prayers for protection. I might have thought authors Neil T. Anderson and Steve Russo were overreacting when I read their book *The Seduction of Our Children* about Satan's schemes to lure our children away from their homes of hope if I hadn't experienced an attack myself. If you don't believe that there is a spiritual battle going on for our children, listen to the lyrics of songs by Marilyn Manson or his predecessor Ozzy Osbourne.

During the years my older son was rebelling, it was easier for me to stay upstairs and assume the best rather than go into his smelly basement room to find out what was really going on in his life. I guess that's why I can begin to understand how the parents of the Columbine shooters didn't know there were shotgun parts in their sons' rooms. When you have a troubled kid, you have to choose your battles. A tidy room is one of the first battles you tend to give up. A neat haircut is another.

But one day my husband-to-be convinced me that it was time for me to pull my head out of the sand and go through Rob's room to find out exactly what was going on in his life. He offered to help, so equipped with trash bags we ventured down the stairs and into the dark bedroom.

We found the usual smelly socks and old pizza boxes, but we also found satanic cult insignia, and poems and drawings more glorifying to the prince of darkness than the God of light. Then I listened to some of the music that I knew was blaring in my son's ears night and day—it was full of messages of destruction, hate, and hopelessness. A steady diet of such evil causes teenage depression at best, suicidal tendencies at worst. I knew without a doubt that we were engaged in a battle for my son's soul.

We cleaned everything questionable out of the room in trash bags that day, barred Satan from the basement of my house in the name of Jesus, and then launched an all-out prayer battle. Satan had set up camp in my basement, but I would not let him have my son. By the grace of God, he did not claim him.

Neil Anderson worked with a teenage girl with a history similar to Rob's. Her name was Kelly. He also used the power of prayer to free her from the negative influences in her life. "You may be surprised to learn that there are many Christian children and teenagers like Kelly populating our schools, attending our churches, and living in our homes," Anderson writes. "They hear inner 'voices' telling them that nobody loves them, urging them to disobey their parents, and disrupting their attempts at Bible reading and prayer. They are the targets of Satan's strategy. He seeks to destroy our families and churches by seducing our children away from their parents and from God."[7]

A home with hope is ever vigilant and alert, praying continuously for God's protection from Satan's schemes against their children. The rights of individuals in the home must be respected, yes. But parents are ordained by God to rule the home, and they have the right to know what's going on within its walls. Again, the Columbine tragedy provides an example. From what I read, it appears Cassie Bernall's parents searched her room and knew it was time to take drastic steps; the killers' parents did not.

The week of the killings at Columbine, Judge Jack DeVita, Magistrate of Jefferson County, Colorado, was interviewed on "Good Morning America." "Parents have a right to sweep their children's room. It's their house," he said unequivocally. Later, I asked Judge DeVita if he received any negative reactions from his comment and he said, "I know many people feel differently, but no one said I was wrong to say what I said in this case. I'm not talking about going through your kid's room every night," he continued. "Some degree of privacy is good. But if you see signs of pot-smoking, pornography, or violence, this gives you an entrée for stepping up your vigilance."

Doing the hard thing, the responsible thing, in times of trouble is one way parents keep the light of hope burning in the windows of their homes and in the hearts of their children. After years of prayer, worship, and modeling of spiritual disciplines and values, God may grant them before they die the privilege of knowing that their children are permanently in His hands through their personal belief in His Son, Jesus Christ.

Even parents determined to establish a home with hope won't always do everything right. There will be fights about who's wearing what to church and who gets to sit in the front seat. There will be graces uttered hastily before meals when at least two people around the table have their mouths full of mashed potatoes. There will be times when other priorities rush in and the spiritual disciplines like quiet time and family worship are left on the shelf to gather dust along with the family Bible. But if there is an honest attempt to create a home with hope, God will honor that effort.

"Let parents be faithful," J. R. Miller writes in his 1912 guide to a strong Christian home. "Let them do their best. The work may seem too great for them, and they may faint under its burdens and seem to fail. But what they cannot do, the angels will come and finish while they sleep. Night by night they will come and correct the day's mistakes, and if need be do all the poor, faulty work over again. Then at last when the parents sleep in death, dropping out of their hands the sacred work they have been doing for their children, again God's angels will come, take up the unfinished work and carry it on to completeness."[8]

That's the kind of legacy left by a home with hope.

♡ Home Builders:

1. Do you live in a home with hope? How are you communicating this hope to your children?

2. Hope grows in the fellowship of believers. How might you strengthen your fellowship commitment at the church you attend?

3. What spiritual disciplines can you practice in order to protect your family from Satan's lies?

A Home with a Family Mission

• • • • • • • • • • • • • •

I know of no realm of life that can provide
more companionship in a lonely world or
greater feelings of security and purpose in
chaotic times than the close ties of a family.

—*Charles R. Swindoll*

One of the most important missions a family has is to
simply be together as a family—resisting the lure of
activities or programs designed for good but resulting
in pulling family members in different directions.

The mission of a family is to create bonds that stretch enough
to allow individual members to explore and become who they
are meant to be, but are also strong enough to pull them back to
that place called home where they will be valued, appreciated,
and encouraged.

What is a family? It can take many forms, of course, but a family is primarily a group of individuals who are related to one
another by marriage, birth, or adoption. Citing a study that was
conducted to determine what makes a healthy family, Charles
Swindoll writes that strong families are those that "are committed
to the family, spend time together, have good family communication,

express appreciation to each other, have a spiritual commitment, and are able to solve problems in a crisis."[1]

What we need to do to build stronger families is make a conscious, purposeful effort at communicating what the mission of a family is. That mission helps each member of the family, from the oldest to the youngest, understand that the family is not merely a group of people who happen to be sharing the same home. Rather it is a group ordained and established by God for the good of all.

Stephen R. Covey, author of several books on effectiveness in people, families, and corporations, encourages families to be so intentional about their union that they actually draft a written family mission statement. Those who have been subjected to long, boring, corporate meetings where every word of a mission statement is debated and challenged may cringe at this suggestion, but it certainly helps in giving focus to family life.

"The core of any family is what is changeless, what is going to be there—shared vision and values," Covey writes. "By writing a family mission statement, you give expression to its true foundation."[2]

And the exercise doesn't have to be boring and interminable. "By getting input from every family member, drafting a statement, getting feedback, revising it, and using wording from different family members, you get the family talking, communicating, on things that really matter deeply," Covey continues.[3] He also advises periodic review of the written statement to keep it updated and says this exercise alone keeps the family united in common values and purposes.

I know that all sounds wonderfully idealistic. You may be thinking that it's enough of a mission just getting your family out the door on time in the morning, equipped with the homework papers or briefcases, lunch money, and jackets they need for the day. Collecting them all back under one roof at the end of the day is the ultimate goal. What happens in between is a blur of sports practices, errands, grocery store express lanes, and self-pump gas stations. How could a family mission statement make any part of the typical day go more smoothly?

Truthfully, a mission statement won't take away the challenges and frustrations of running a family. But it can give everyone in the family a sense that everything they do contributes in some way to the good of the family and the individuals in it. It can also give them the assurance that the family will survive regardless of what happens on any single hectic day.

As a writer of sentiments for greeting cards and gifts, I've noticed several popular statements sold on wall plaques that could be termed family mission statements. No doubt people see them and say, "that sounds like our family too." A best-selling family mission statement from direct marketer Abbey Press reads:

IN THIS HOME
We believe in living deeply,
laughing often and loving always.
We believe we were brought together
to support and care for each other.
We believe in celebrating together—
our faith, our heritage,
our traditions.
We believe that everyone's feelings count,
and that the uniqueness of each of us
strengthens all of us.
We believe
in the power of forgiveness to heal
and the power of love
to carry us through.
We believe in one another,
in this family,
IN THIS HOME. [4]

Your family could adopt this statement or write one tailored to your beliefs and values. One reflecting more dependence on God, for instance, might read: "The mission of this family is simple, Lord. Because You love us, we will love one another. Because we love one another, we will also reach out to love others."

Author and speaker Kendra Smiley and her husband have raised three sons on their farm in Illinois. While her family doesn't have a written mission statement, she says "we all know that our goal as a family is to live in such a way that others can see Jesus Christ in us."

Jill Savage, founder of the Hearts at Home ministry, says her family is still in the process of finalizing their mission statement, but it will probably go something like this: "The Savage family exists to glorify God, build one another up, and build into the lives that intersect with our family."

Whatever a family's mission is, it serves as a standard against which all decisions and actions can be measured. Is spending beyond your means in keeping with your mission as a family? Is offering someone in transition a place to stay a part of your mission? Why or why not?

It takes a home with a mission, written or understood, to provide families with the direction and grounding they need to move out into the world confidently and return home gladly at the end of the day.

Families in Focus

One of the pastors at our church preached a sermon titled "What is a Family?" In it he pointed out that sometimes looking at the mistakes and misconceptions about family can help us discern what is right and true instead.

While a balanced family provides a place for us to love and grow, a family that is out of balance may reveal individuals with a sense of selfishness and lack of respect for other family members.

Neglect can occur when someone in the family, especially a parent, begins living as if the family doesn't matter. To the other extreme, the sin of idolatry is present when one makes the family his or her entire identity.

A sick family is characterized by closed systems in which members are forced to play unchanging roles. It may have rigid rules, but no guidelines. It keeps many secrets, provides little privacy, and offers no encouragement. In the worst cases, verbal or physical abuse is also a regular part of family life.

By contrast, communication, listening, affirmation, and support characterize a healthy family. Respect and trust are ever present in a home where a family is living out its intended purpose. So is a sense of humor and balanced interaction between family members. A healthy family has shared responsibilities and shared spiritual values. It respects privacy, admits problems, and celebrates family traditions. It's a home with a mission.

Once the family understands that family life matters and will be given priority by everyone involved, it's easier for each individual to see how he or she fits into the overall mission. A home with a family mission is a home in which parents can be parents and children can be children as each does his or her part.

"Families these days tend to be child-centered . . . everything revolves around the children," writes John MacArthur in his book *Successful Christian Parenting.* "The children's activities, their relationships and their interests tend to set the family agenda. But God's design for family is that it be first Christ-centered, and then marriage-centered, with the husband-wife relationship taking priority over all other relationships in the home and the parents, not the children, determining the family agenda."[5]

The Marriage-Centered Family

In chapter seven we discussed how Christ-centered families that worship and pray together live in homes with hope. Whatever tragedy or problem situation a family must face, doing so with Jesus Christ at the center of every decision, and turning to the Bible for the "how-to" information needed on a daily basis, will ensure that this first priority of a healthy family is established.

But how does being marriage-centered help a family fulfill its mission? If the family includes a married couple, the marriage has to be in second place in terms of importance in the home. God began His concept of families by putting man and woman together in marriage. He will honor and bless those homes that honor and bless His ordained relationship. Besides, if a marriage isn't strong, the family is far more vulnerable to being torn apart by divorce and separation.

There are few terms more painful to a divorced parent than the term "broken home." A divorced parent already feels as if everyone else in the world is in perfect Norman Rockwell families, and while it's descriptive, the term "broken home" rubs salt in the wound.

At least that's how I felt after my divorce. Even going grocery shopping those first few weeks was extremely painful for me. First of all, I felt as if I had a giant D for divorced emblazoned on my forehead. Although I'm a naturally extroverted, gregarious person, I would actually pass by an aisle in the grocery store if I saw someone I knew standing there. I wanted to avoid having to talk to them.

As if pushing a shopping cart with all that heaviness in my heart wasn't hard enough, inevitably I would see headlines about "broken homes" or "kids from broken families" leaping off the covers of periodicals at the checkout stand.

In a sense, I suppose children of divorce do live in broken homes, but homes with two parents in residence can be broken too if the marriage is not a healthy one and both partners fail to make marriage a priority second only to their focus on Jesus Christ. This is confirmed time and again when couples faced with the empty nest look at one another and realize that without the children to give them a common purpose, they have forgotten how to live together as man and wife.

In a home with a family mission that includes the right of parents to be parents and children to be children, the parents work hard at keeping their marriages alive. They develop ways of communicating effectively, and they learn the art of successful compromise. They also learn to fight fairly and recover from disagreements quickly—and they "do not let the sun go down" while they are still angry (Eph. 4:26). The wise couple also knows how important it is to keep their relationship not only cooking . . . but sizzling.

The book *Intimate Issues,* by Linda Dillow and Lorraine Pintus, is full of real-life advice on how to keep marriages alive and well. I laughed out loud when I read the chapter titled, "How Do I Make Love with Children Wrapped Around My Knees?" The tendency of many couples with a house full of preschoolers is to just put off focusing on the sexual part of their marriage relationship until the kids are older, but that sage Ann Landers advice to "use it or lose it" certainly applies here. Marriage counselors have stated that any part of a marriage that disappears due to neglect is not likely to come back another time.

"We must pay attention," the authors of *Intimate Issues* state. "We do not have to live as if there is no tomorrow, but we had better love creatively as though there is only now."[6] The book goes on to suggest a bedroom rendezvous, a home date, or a planned escape together to keep romance alive. The goal is to make sure the couple has private "married" time when they can enjoy the fragrances of perfume and after-shave instead of being constantly surrounded by the aroma of dirty diapers.

Will there be time to renew the marriage once the kids get married? Sure there will be. But unless the home is marriage-centered all along, there won't be much heat in the embers you hope to re-ignite. Whether it's written down or just understood, "marriage matters" needs to be a part of every family mission. Not only to preserve the marriage of the parents in the home, but to model for the children what it means to be a dedicated husband or wife who is willing to make personal sacrifices for the sake of the marriage.

Single parents may have a harder time providing an example of a healthy marriage to their children, but they can still do it. Often there are grandparents with a long-term, committed marriage, or neighbors and friends that a single mom can hold up to her children as examples of what a healthy marriage looks like.

In 1993, Jill Savage gave birth to Hearts at Home, her ministry to stay-at-home moms. Her desire to "professionalize" motherhood resulted in the evolution of the ministry to one with national focus and conferences drawing as many as five thousand moms at once. When asked about her own home life, however, Jill admits that she and her husband, Mark, who have four children, have experienced many ups and downs during the fifteen years of their marriage.

"We've had to learn how to serve each other," Jill responded to the question about her relationship with Mark now. "What we've discovered is that when you place the needs of the other one first, your own needs are going to be met. And we've learned to trust. God's so good—He's restored what we knew could happen. But we had to work really hard to get there."[7]

I asked Jill if she feels her children notice the sacrifices she and Mark make for the sake of their marriage, and she told me they do because they see their parents giving up personal time to make time together a priority each day.

"As soon as Mark gets home in the evening, he kisses the kids and then he and I take about fifteen minutes to have what we call 'kitchen time' together," Jill explained. "We both might have other things we want to do, but we make getting together our first priority. This is our time to connect. It's also a time to ask 'what do you need this evening?' so we can make sure we don't have separate agendas pulling us in different directions. The kids understand that barring a crisis, we are going to have this time together. They respect our need for 'kitchen time,' and it's a daily reminder to them of how much we value our marriage."

When children see parents making time for one another, and making sacrifices for the good of the family, they realize that their parents really believe what they teach about values and what matters most in life. Sometimes the sacrifice takes the form of turning down a higher paying job, a position with more prestige, or a promotion requiring more time away from home.

A couple in our community held highly visible jobs as co-anchors on a local television station when they decided to chuck it all and go into real estate together in order to have more time with their two young children.

"I wanted to send a strong message to our kids that self-worth is not determined by how much money you make and how well known you are," the children's mother said.

There has to be more than a little give and take, but in a healthy family the needs of everyone will eventually be addressed and met if possible. Everyone in the family needs Christ, and a husband and wife need one another. Once those relationships are soundly established, it will be much more likely that the children's needs will be met too.

Meeting Children's Needs

What do children need most?

Parents and experts I've consulted agree that children need to feel blessed and loved by their parents—to know that they have someone in this world whom they can count on no matter what and who will love them unconditionally. They also need to feel that they fulfill a special role in the family and world in which they find themselves.

Children also need to know that there is something they can do better than average. Whether it's playing a trombone or doing a double back flip, they're good at it and they know it. Most of all, they need to have a clear sense of their worth in God's eyes, along with a growing, personal relationship with Him. The family that can lead a child toward getting all those needs met has fulfilled its mission well. The reward will be happy, productive young adults who eventually move out in the world to raise their own God-centered families.

Of course, meeting those needs isn't always easy. Philosophically, we can probably all agree that we want to give our children this strong foundation, but some needs are easier to provide than others.

Love and support come fairly naturally for most parents. God plants in our hearts the ability to love our children unconditionally at about the same time He begins creating them in the womb. Parents expecting their second child often wonder if they will be able to love the new baby as much as they love their firstborn, but they soon realize that their capacity to love simply doubles as part of God's plan.

We parents can usually do a pretty good job of being supportive and of delivering the "you are special and unique, there's no one just like you" message. Where it gets tougher is in knowing when we should intentionally lead children into activities that develop their skills, talents, and interests—and when we have simply pushed too hard for too long.

When things are going well, we aren't likely to second-guess our decisions. But when one child is acting out, or becomes a full-fledged prodigal, the "what ifs" can be brutal.

A strong family includes in its mission the flexibility to support one another through changes, even the painful ones. The goal is not to sacrifice the family in the process, but to keep the bonds of protection around the person in transition as lovingly and firmly as possible.

Carolyn Lewis was the founding director of the Parenting Guidance Center in Richmond, Indiana. Now retired, she often volunteers to share her knowledge about successful parenting with young parents and families.

"The family is the most stable unit of our society," Lewis says, "yet it is always changing: weddings, adoptions, the addition of in-laws and various loss experiences impact the family unit. By making healthy adjustments to change, the family becomes the basic problem-solving unit in our society."

Lewis's tried and true philosophy of parenting is basic and effective. She encourages parents to think of their role in two parts: care giving and role modeling. "Care giving is what we do," she states. "Role modeling is who we are. Care giving plus role modeling equals love."

"God sets the lonely in families," the Bible states in Psalm 68:6. We can only hope that those He sets in our family won't ever feel lonely or unwanted, but it can happen.

When the teenage years arrive, the happy children you've nurtured and given plenty of playtime, the ones you've taught to roll with the changes and pursue their talents and skills, can become like strangers to the family. They can even put up a sort of screen to keep you away.

The last group of such teenagers I spotted was hanging out in front of a movie theater. With their multicolored spiked hair, their tattoos, and their pierced body parts, they were the latest version of the "teen screen."

Every generation has had a group of teens who chose to dress and act differently from the rest. The elements used to create the screen really don't matter. What difference does it make if the hair is blue or orange? Or if the ear or the navel is pierced? What stays the same is that the outrageously dressed teenager is saying, "I dare you to see who I really am." Without knowing it, he or she is also saying, "please care enough to look beyond my screen."

I believe that the teenagers who throw up the screens need more attention than the more "normal-looking" kids. Something has hurt them. The screen is built out of anger, confusion, or rejection and is designed to shield them from any more hurt.

The best educators, psychologists, and youth workers know the screen is temporary. They try to see through it to recognize and affirm the teenager behind it before self-destruction takes over. These people are worth a hundred times what they are paid.

Other professionals find it easier to slap a label on the unconventional teen and look away, focusing instead on the model kids. The damage they do by being so quick to label is a hundred times more destructive than they realize.

It's so important for those of us who come upon a teen screen to look beyond it, whether the teen is a member of our family or just someone we happen to see. If I pass a teenager with green hair and a pierced nose at the mall, I say good morning and look him or her in the eye just as I would any other shopper. I want to be the mirror that says, "I see you in there, and you deserve to be recognized."

When a teenager decides to throw up a screen, it can be hard on everyone in the family. But it's also the family that can give her the courage to drop the screen and go on to become the person she is meant to be.

I'm convinced that kids behind the screen need at least one person who remembers when they dressed dolls or built a fort out of scraps of wood. Someone who watched them blow out birthday candles. Someone who knows the real person behind the screen, and who's ready to do whatever it takes to get that person back again.

I learned all this the hard way. My older son threw up a very effective screen during his adolescence. Gratefully, he turned away from self-destruction, supported by the prayers and "tough love" of several people in his life, before it was too late.

Long after my son chose to come out from behind his screen, after he was a college graduate, a sensitive husband, and a caring father, he turned to me one day and asked, "Mom, why didn't you give up on me back then?"

"Because moms never give up," I said. And neither should families.

If you know a teenager hiding behind a screen, don't give up. Get as tough as you have to, but always be a mirror reflecting who you know he or she really is, because every single one of them is worth recognizing and saving.

It helps to draw on the knowledge of experts. A national organization called Assets for Youth has identified forty assets that child care experts agree are necessary for children to grow into caring adults. Those assets range from caring families and neighborhoods to self-esteem, self-restraint, the motivation to achieve, even how much time they spend reading. They are conducting surveys of more than ninety thousand teenagers and middle-schoolers nationwide to find out if the kids believe these assets are present in their lives. Many do not. The results are eye opening for parents, families, and school systems, and a good place to start when you want to reach a troubled child.

Of all the kids interviewed, 36 percent said they didn't feel they had the support of their families, and only 50 percent said their families set limits on their behavior. Just 55 percent said they felt safe in their hometowns.[8] When the survey results are released in each community, surveyors make a point of saying the community needs to step up and meet the needs of kids who aren't getting their needs met at home. But wouldn't it be so much better for families, kids, and communities if they did get what they needed at home?[9]

And issues that only used to concern parents of teenagers now concern parents of much younger children.

Columnist Suzanne Fields estimates there are 15.4 million American girls between the ages of five and twelve creating a "huge market for lip gloss, roll-on glitter, nail polish in berry flavors and scented packages that swiftly graduate to bizarre colors and vulgar

exaggeration."[10] This isn't the teen market; it's the tween market—
and isn't it horrifying to note that marketers now say it begins at age
five. Though chronologically midway between early childhood and
adolescence, this group is leaning more and more toward teen
styles, teen attitudes, and sadly, teen behavior at its most troubling.

What has experts and parents concerned is that behaviors
exhibited by sixteen-year-old girls not so long ago are now evidenced in girls ten years old and even younger.

I experienced this phenomenon firsthand when our two oldest granddaughters turned six and eight on the same weekend
and had a joint birthday party at a pizza parlor. Riding to the
party I was in a car with a group of the five and six year olds.
They were telling corny jokes, elbowing one another, and giggling
a lot, just as you might expect.

Riding home with the eight year olds, the conversation was
much different. They knew and could sing every word of songs by
The Backstreet Boys. What will they be doing by the time they are
ten? My son and his wife discourage the teenage behaviors, and
recognize and encourage the more age-appropriate ones. But it
takes strong parents aware of their mission to do that.

"More and more we see adolescent clothes, attitudes, and values being marketed to younger and younger children," Dr. James
Dobson wrote. "This adolescent obsession can place our children
on a very unnatural timetable, likely to reach the peak of sexual
interest several years before it's due. That has obvious implications
for their social and emotional health. . . . Therefore, I strongly rec-
ommend that parents screen the influences to which their children
are exposed, keeping activities appropriate for each age," Dobson
continues. "While we can't isolate our kids from the world as it is,
we don't have to turn our babies into teenyboppers."[11]

With these and many more societal pressures coming into
play, even strong families will have their ups and downs. There
will be disappointments, challenges, and disasters that seem to

shake the family to its core. But there will also be enough grace to forgive, and enough love to keep a sense of family mission alive even in the midst of childhood disasters or teenage turmoil.

God's Family

At the beginning of this chapter we defined a family as primarily a group of individuals who are related to one another by marriage, birth, or adoption. In that same sense, we can all be a part of God's family too. When we accept Jesus Christ as Lord and Savior, we are "born again" into the family of God. Paul writing to the Romans encouraged them by saying, "The Spirit himself testifies with our spirit that we are God's children. Now if we are children, then we are heirs—heirs of God and co-heirs with Christ, if indeed we share in his sufferings in order that we may also share in his glory" (Rom. 8:16-17).

God promised us that He would be our God and we would be His people. "I will be a Father to you, and you will be my sons and daughters, says the Lord Almighty" (2 Cor. 6:18).

Our earthly families may disappoint us in a hundred thousand ways. They may even become "broken." But being a member of God's family means that we will always have a cord pulling us toward His love and forgiveness—pulling us toward the place where we will be valued, appreciated, and encouraged.

As blended families go, ours has been as tension free as any. For the most part, all the parents and stepparents involved get along, and gratefully, the children seem to have moved beyond the pain of divorce to live productive, happy lives. Still, the consequences of divorce go on and on.

My second husband and I are blessed to have one another and we know it. We won't ever take our marriage for granted because we know that it is a gift from the hand of a forgiving, gracious God. As happy as we are to be remarried, however, we will both always feel the hurt of having lost the original family units into which our children were born. Every holiday, every milestone occasion reminds us once again of the history we have lost, and of the consequences of operating outside of God's plan for the families He created.

This is especially true now that grandchildren are being born into our blended family. All four of our children are married and we have six grandchildren with one on the way as I write this. Those precious little ones are the fulfillment of God's promise to exchange "beauty for ashes," and we love them dearly. But as joyful as each new birth is, it's sad that Jim and I can't experience the joy together the way we would if we could turn to one another and say, "Oh, she looks just like her mother when she was first born, remember?"

What we've learned to do in our family is make the best of every situation and shower one another with an awful lot of grace and forgiveness. A little divine intervention helps too.

One Sunday I was upset about some reality of our blended family situation. Since the Lord has taught me to only go to my husband with problems he can solve, but to go to Him with everything else, I was praying for a solution. What I temporarily forgot is that while we are forgiven for past mistakes, our just and righteous God does not remove the consequences of our actions. In short, there would be no solution for my problem.

But as I took my disappointment to the Lord, I heard His answer loud and clear. First, I heard Him gently but firmly remind me that He had blessed me with a second husband and a wonderful Christian marriage—something He didn't have to do but did out of His grace and love for me. Secondly, I seemed to hear Him say, "Besides, isn't being a part of My family enough for you?"

"Yes, Lord," I responded quietly in my heart. "Of course it is." Since that day I've been able to let go of many small disappointments before they became bigger hurts. After all, I already have a perfect family—I'm a daughter of the King.

"Our true family is the family of God," said Dr. Henry Cloud and Dr. John Townsend in their book *Boundaries*. "In this family, which is to be our strongest tie, things are done a certain way. We are to tell the truth, set limits, take and require responsibility, confront each other, forgive each other, and so on. Strong standards and values make this family run. And God will not allow it any other way in his family."[12]

As we look at our earthly families and how they are running, we can be encouraged if we remember first and foremost that we are a part of God's family. Each one of us is already unconditionally loved, accepted, and valued in His eyes, because Jesus paid the price for our sins. Our attempts to create a home with a strong family mission will be less than perfect, but we have to keep trying because our efforts can lead our children to accept their place in God's family. And then they will have the best home of all.

Home Builders:

1. What are some elements you might include in your Family Mission Statement? (HINT: Find the common threads, things that are important to all family members.)
2. What drives your family life? Is it God centered, marriage centered, and child centered in that order? What are some shifts that you might need to make to balance the equation?
3. If you've accepted Jesus Christ as your Lord and Savior, you are a member of God's family. What's your role in this family? (If you haven't accepted Jesus, why not do it now? Just tell Him you believe He is the Son of God and declare your need for Him to be your Savior. Confess your sins to Him and ask for His forgiveness, and He will welcome you into His family this very moment!)

A Home with Open Doors

• • • • • • • • • • • • • • • •

The glory of the house is hospitality.

—*Fireplace Motto*

The home of a welcoming family is a wonderful place to visit. Such a home reaches out to embrace and minister to others, whether it's to extended family or to the weary traveler passing through town.

"The ornament of a house is the friends who frequent it," Emerson wrote. Certainly a secure home is one that invites not only friends to come in, but international students, community groups, and other families as well. When a family reaches out to others, children are enriched with a sense of a larger world than the one they know. A world waiting for them to take their place in it.

"I live in a very small house," reads a Chinese proverb, "but my window looks out on a very large world." It takes a home with wide windows and open doors to help children develop a global worldview. Such a home is open to admitting people different from those in the family and to learning about people of other cultures, as well as the poor and the aging of all races in our own culture. It's a home that best prepares children for healthy lives unfettered by the chains of prejudice and bias.

There were many wonderful, stabilizing things about growing up in the same house all through my childhood. That I can still visit my original home now is a gift I've never taken for granted. But such a provincial existence didn't do much to give my sisters and me a worldview beyond East Tennessee. We all went to the same schools and church. My parents' friends, for the most part, were people they met in college in the same town. We always shopped at the same grocery store and celebrated family occasions in the same downtown restaurant. Stable? Yes. Conducive to expanding our horizons? Not really.

But one day my parents made a decision to shake things up a bit. In their wisdom, they realized both the benefits and the limitations of the stable environment in which they were raising their daughters, so they volunteered to have a foreign exchange student stay in our home for the summer.

Now you must realize that to three young girls born and raised in the South, a visitor from any place north of Kentucky would have seemed like a foreigner. After all, we would have thought that they talked funny, wore weird clothes, and preferred strange foods—all characteristics of a multicultural experience.

I still remember the first day Martine, sixteen, came to stay with us. I was thirteen, my sister Patty was seventeen, and my younger sister Mary was nine. I'm absolutely sure all three of us girls stared at Martine all through dinner, and whatever fried dish my mother had prepared as her welcome meal was left untouched on our plates.

The most romantic, intriguing city we could imagine in all the world was Paris, France, and Martine was from Paris. I can still remember her dark, coarse hair and bushy eyebrows, and her purplish fingernail polish. She wore a lot of black: black sweaters and tight black slacks. Since girls in the South in those days seldom wore black until they were married, she seemed sophisticated and glamorous to us. She even smelled glamorous, as a cloud of French perfume followed her wherever she went and lingered behind whenever she had passed through a room.

Martine loved to accompany my mother to the grocery store where she marveled at the size of the store and all the choices we had. Maybe she also went in hope of finding more things she would like to eat. My dad had a huge vegetable garden, and the summer Martine was with us was a banner year for corn. We had corn-on-the-cob almost every night, and I think it was several weeks into Martine's visit before she worked up the courage to say, "I do not like zee corn."

What we didn't suspect about Martine when we first met her was that she would have a lot of the same feelings we would have if we were so far from home. She asked my mother to make some of her favorite French dishes, and she taught us some French words (which we spoke with a Tennessee accent) so she could hear her native language occasionally. One day I found her sitting in the kitchen talking to my mother and crying—because she was homesick. Other times we'd sit up in our pajamas and talk and laugh on Martine's bed. By the time she returned to Paris at the end of the summer, we realized she was far more like us than she was different. And we missed her terribly.

Opportunities to have students from other countries stay in American homes weren't as plentiful in the '60s as they are today. Christian ministries offering exchange programs abound because as Tom Phillips, president and CEO of International Students, Inc. (ISI), told me, "Other countries send their best and brightest to the United States. Sponsoring one of these students, inviting them to visit their homes and exposing them to a family focused on Jesus Christ, may be the best chance many families have to impact the world for Christianity."

The likelihood is that these bright, talented young people will return to their home countries and be in positions of influence. This was certainly true of Corazon Aquino, former president of the Republic of the Philippines, and Benjamin Netanyahu, prime minister of Israel, both of whom attended college in the U.S. In fact, according to ISI, America hosts the largest number of internationals of any country, with over 550,000 international students and scholars from 188 countries studying here. Most of the students are from Asia (57.3 percent), followed by Europe (14.8 percent) and Latin America (10.4 percent).[1]

But when a family opens its doors to just one exchange student, the extent of the program doesn't matter nearly as much as creating a welcoming environment. If the program includes providing a residence, just finding a little elbow room for one more person is the key. The family that hosts may be impacted and changed as much as the guest who stays.

Such was the experience of the Stringfellow family in Colorado Springs when they accepted a high school student to live with them for eleven months.

"When I think back to my growing-up years, it seemed we always had someone extra living with us," Carolyn Stringfellow said. "I guess that's why it seems natural to me now for our family to take in anyone who needs a place to stay for any reason."

The Stringfellows had a teenage daughter and son, one a senior and the other a sophomore, when the call came asking them if they would consider taking an exchange student from Bishkek, Kyrgzstan, a former Soviet state now a small independent country.

"The person who called said that two people had recommended us," Carolyn told me. "We had to discuss it, pray about it, and agree as a family that we wanted to do it, but in the end we all believed the Lord wanted us to say yes, and so we did."

Kyrgzstan is a Muslim country that also experienced fifty years of communist rule, so the Stringfellows assumed that their student, who Americanized her name to Helen, would not be a Christian. However, because their teenagers were attending a Christian school, Helen did also. The day Carolyn took Helen in to meet the music director and audition for a singing group called Witness, she overheard the teacher telling Helen that one of the requirements for being in the program was to share her story of how she came to know Jesus.

Carolyn whisked Helen away, explaining to the teacher that they would have to talk about Jesus at home and Helen would get back to her. Imagine Carolyn's surprise when she began to explain what it meant to have a relationship with the Lord to Helen and Helen said, "I know about Jesus. My art teacher in school told me about Him and now I am the only Christian in my family."

Later that school year the seniors were in a Bible class when a video was shown of Christians in former Soviet countries. "That's my church in Kyrgzstan!" Helen exclaimed. "I know those people!"

Obviously, Helen's placement in what was to her an obscure place called Colorado Springs, Colorado, was meant to be. Her hometown of Bishkek seemed like an obscure place to the Stringfellows, but the better they got to know Helen, the more obvious it became that the two sister cities were connected at heart, and Helen's placement truly had been a "God thing."

In her year with the Stringfellows, Helen also went to church with her American family and had many opportunities to grow in her faith that she might not have had in her own country. The Stringfellow teenagers grew from the experience too.

"Because of our having Helen with us, and also because we've been able to go on missions trips with our two kids, I can see both of them beginning to show interest in the mission field too," Carolyn said. "It's hard for me to think of them being far away from home, but I know if it's the Lord's will for them to go, then it will be okay."

Hosting an exchange student is just one way homes with open doors can expose their children to other cultures. Not all families can travel internationally, but one positive aspect of children having access to the Internet and television is that they truly get a broader understanding of diverse cultures. Families with limited space and small budgets can still invite international people visiting their churches to their homes for coffee and cake. Trips to the library can introduce children to different cultures too.

Embracing Diversity

While I continue to believe in diversity, the word itself has become such a loaded one for me that I tend to use it cautiously. It seems the slogan Celebrate Diversity, in itself a positive concept, has come to mean celebrate homosexuality, abortion, and every cult and religion except Christianity. However, Christians are called to embrace diversity. We are citizens of the world by virtue of the fact that we follow Jesus Christ and He told us to, "Go and make disciples of all nations, baptizing them in the name of the Father, and of the Son and of the Holy Spirit" (Matt. 28:19).

"Red and yellow, black and white, they are precious in His sight," the little children sing. The hatred still evidenced by the racism and bigotry in our country is a sickness for which there often seems to be no cure. We must teach our children the truth about diversity—that all people are equally loved and valued in God's eyes—if we are to have any hope of teaching them to love their neighbors as themselves. It's not just an option for Christians.

A song in the musical *South Pacific* addresses the fact that bigotry and prejudice are not necessarily innate, but "have to be carefully taught." On the other hand, efforts to expose children to healthy multicultural experiences will increase their ability to be citizens of the world Jesus loves. Encouraging children to have open minds is every bit as important as raising them in a home with open doors.

And it's never too early for us to begin exposing children to diverse cultures. Elisa Morgan, president of MOPS International, encourages mothers of preschoolers to work with their toddlers to help them understand that not everyone lives or looks exactly as they do. One idea she suggests is to teach them about holidays celebrated by different ethnic groups.

"Childhood curiosity about diversity in our world is natural and healthy," Morgan said. "By teaching our children to celebrate diversity rather than fear it, we broaden their horizons and open doors to possibilities for us all."[2]

Another way to introduce diversity to children is to tell them about their own heritage. Especially in the United States, most everyone can trace family roots back two or three hundred years to discover forefathers and foremothers of Irish, German, African, and other descents.

"Many Americans are historians without being aware of it," says William R. Ferris, chairman of the National Endowment for the Humanities. "Each of us has stories we pass on, like family heirlooms, from generation to generation."[3]

If we don't tell our children about our childhoods and the stories our grandparents told us, then who will? Telling them about all the obstacles and successes we've had in getting to the age we are today also is a way of passing on family history.

I was blessed to have a dad who made a point of telling us all about our heritage when we were growing up. Both his mother and father were descendents of French-Swiss immigrants who settled in East Tennessee, and my father became the keeper of memoirs, photographs and other memorabilia from the French-Swiss. He also restored the home his grandparents built and succeeded in having it listed in the National Register of Historic Sites.

I recently wrote a juvenile historical fiction novel, *The Journey of Elisa,* based on the memoirs of my great-grandmother, Elisa Bolli Buffat. When I read the manuscript to my two eldest granddaughters, they became totally fascinated with Elisa. They loved seeing the old photographs of her and her family and touching the old French Bible that was given to her when she was eleven. Looking at their faces as we sorted through the photos together, I realized they actually resembled Elisa.

Francesca and Amanda have an Hispanic mother (my daughter-in-law Maria), so they are a blend of French and Spanish heritage, among others. It's our hope as their parents and grandparents that if we help them to embrace their rich, multicultural heritage, they will be more accepting of diversity in other people.

The Christian Worldview

Why does it matter? Why isn't it enough that we take our children to church and help them with their homework? If we also work hard at our jobs, provide a good living for our families, go to Bible studies and fellowship with other Christians, aren't we living the life the Lord would want us to live?

Yes and no. The danger in Christian circles today is that we don't believe we can change this post-Christian culture where Judeo-Christian values are no longer the basis for ethical and moral decisions in our society. Instead, we turn our hearts and minds inward. We surround ourselves only with other Christians, shaking our heads as we walk into church with our designer Bible covers and pledge envelopes, convinced that keeping our own family safe is all we can do.

But into this padded pew existence comes the voice of Chuck Colson, whom many view as a modern-day prophet. Former Watergate conspirator, born again Christian, and founder of Prison Fellowship, Colson is becoming increasingly intense in his writing and teaching about the worldview Christians are called to adopt.

In the millenium book he wrote with Nancy Pearcey, *How Now Shall We Live?*, Colson explains what a worldview is, and why Christianity is one.

"The term *worldview* may sound abstract or philosophical, a topic discussed by pipe-smoking, tweed-jacketed professors in academic settings. But actually a person's worldview is intensely practical. It is simply the sum total of our beliefs about the world, the 'big picture' that directs our daily decisions and actions. And understanding worldviews is extremely important."[4]

Colson explains that our choices are shaped by our beliefs about what is real and true, right and wrong, good and beautiful. Our choices are shaped by our worldview. The basis for the Christian worldview is what we know to be real and true through biblical revelation. Biblical accounts of Creation, the Fall, and redemption through Jesus Christ constitute the truth to which Christians cling.

"We are compelled to see Christianity as the all-encompassing truth, the root of everything else," Colson writes. "It is ultimate reality."[5]

To have a global worldview is to apply what we know and believe to be true to all people wherever they live, regardless of religious or cultural differences. Jesus asked His followers not just to meet and tend to people in a physical way, spreading the good news of the gospel, but to go where they were philosophically as well. We must develop the desire to do so in our children as well as in ourselves.

It's not always comfortable to live out our Christian worldview, either by giving up modern comfort by going to Third World countries or by going across town to a gathering where you know you will be the only Christian in the room. My husband and I have been considering joining a group in our community called Food for Thought, the sole purpose of which is to bring together people with diverse beliefs for discussion and a meal at one member's home. Topics are tossed out on the table along with the potluck dishes, and rules for civil disagreement are agreed to in advance. Still, it's a scary proposition.

Application for membership in this group means you have to give yourselves a label philosophically. Our label would be evangelical Christian, making us targets for attack in a city where the lines of spiritual warfare are pretty clearly drawn—but also giving us an excellent opportunity to spread the Christian worldview.

We know two couples who participate in Food for Thought, and we've been told that even proclaimed witches are seated at the table. We tell ourselves it's a scheduling problem preventing us from joining, but as I write this I wonder if we're just avoiding something potentially difficult. We have Christian friends whom we rarely have time to see, we can rationalize. Shouldn't we spend any extra time we have with them instead?

Yet a Food for Thought table is just the kind of place Jesus would have chosen to dine, isn't it? In his book *The Jesus I Never Knew*, Philip Yancey says, "Jesus was 'the man for others,' in Bonhoeffer's fine phrase. He kept himself free—free for the other person. He would accept almost anybody's invitation to dinner, and as a result no public figure had a more diverse list of friends, ranging from rich people, Roman centurions, and Pharisees to tax collectors, prostitutes, and leprosy victims. People *liked* being with Jesus; where he was, joy was."[6]

Paul, too, never chose the easy path, but made sure his ministry included places like Athens and Ephesus, hotbeds of immorality and pagan worship.

In a home with open doors, opportunities to entertain people of different beliefs are embraced, and children learn at a young age that with the truth they know and live, they can change the world, one life at a time.

For many years we have sponsored children through the Compassion International program. Three of the photos on the side of our refrigerator, mixed in with snapshots of our own kids and grandkids, are of the three Compassion children we sponsored until they graduated from the program.

On the front of the refrigerator are our two new Compassion children, Alavala of India, and Amizo of the Democratic Republic of Congo. Alavala stands demurely in her photo wearing a bright pink dress she must have borrowed from an older sister because it's far too big for her. Amizo stands facing the camera with a scowl on his little face and, one has to suspect from his expression, a chip on his eight-year-old shoulder.

Whenever Francesca and Amanda come to visit they always pay special attention to the photos of Alavala and Amizo. They ask me questions about their lives and how they spend the money we send them each month. When I told them one of our former Compassion children spent her birthday money on vitamins for her younger sister and a goat for her family, they were amazed. They may not have a global worldview yet, but they've gotten a "world peek."

These two little girls have also learned a lot about different lifestyles by coming to visit us in the "big city" from the rural San Luis Valley in southwest Colorado where they live. One summer when they were here for two weeks at "Camp Grancy and Papa," we were stopped at a traffic light when they noticed some homeless people standing on the corner holding up signs asking for food and money.

"Who are those people?" Francesca asked. She could read well enough to make out some of the words on the sign and knew they were asking for help. What followed was the best explanation I could give about the homeless populations in the cities and how we can best help by supporting the shelters and programs that ensure the money goes to helping them turn their lives around.

But does any Christian ever sit at a traffic light, see people holding up signs begging for money, and not wonder what Christ would do? I knew my "politically correct" answer to the girls as to why I didn't give the people money that day hadn't satisfied them when I observed them later that afternoon.

They were playing in the family room and had tossed a blanket over an end table, enabling them to hide inside a makeshift tent. Outside the tent was a sign they had made which read:

"Homless. Pleeze help." The message they were sending to me, whether they knew it or not, was, "If we were homeless, Grancy, would you help us?"

We have to let the Spirit lead us. One Sunday close to Christmas, friends of ours saw a shabbily dressed man and woman sitting in the back of the large Sunday School class they attend. The woman was holding a small baby wrapped in blankets. As our friends walked past, the man asked if it would be possible for them to help his family. It seemed their car needed repair, and they needed a ride back to the run-down motel where they were staying.

"We weren't sure whether it was safe for us to get involved or not," my friend Jane said, "especially since we had our kids with us. But we trusted the message we seemed to be getting from the Holy Spirit, and they piled into our car."

Before taking the family home, our friends took them to the grocery store to buy some basic food and supplies for the baby. Then they gave them one hundred dollars for car repairs and let them out at the motel. The man promised to return the money, but never did.

"It really doesn't matter," Jane said. "We felt we were doing what we were supposed to do to help, and it was a wonderful experience for our children to be a part of reaching out to others. Especially since it was Christmastime and that family reminded us of the one who found no room at the inn so long ago."

My mom has her own way of dealing with the homeless problem. On the land surrounding the big old farm where I grew up and she still lives, there are several small houses we loosely refer to as her "rental properties." Mom's criteria for screening renters aren't the most exhaustive. If the inquirers look her in the eye and shake her hand, and she basically gets a good feeling about them, she'll let them rent one of these houses. More often than not, the renters pay for a month or two, then drop by for a cup of coffee and regale my mother with all the extenuating circumstances preventing them from coming up with the rent money that month.

My mother never thinks of evicting these people as long as they keep up the property and don't cause any trouble. "I know you'll pay when you can," she responds. It's a standing joke in our family about mom and her renters. Cecil, a dear family friend, tells my mother, "If I ever have to rent, I sure hope I can rent from you!" I suspect some of these people have taken advantage of my mother's generosity, but once when I was visiting, one of the renters dropped by with cash for back rent. I saw the look of gratitude on his face as he talked to my mom. What she has is her own non-profit agency for the homeless—without the tax advantages.

Whether it's the homeless problem, or any number of needs worldwide, our own hearts and our children's hearts respond more readily whenever we become aware of how the problem is affecting children.

One Thanksgiving, columnist Ina Hughes, who now writes for the *Knoxville News-Sentinel*, wrote a prayer for children as her column offering for *The Charlotte Observer*. She was overwhelmed by the response it received. It's been used in schools and churches all over the country, and has been reprinted in countless editorial columns and other publications. I knew it had reached classic status when I saw it circulated on e-mail recently attributed to "anonymous."

"We pray for children who want to be carried and for those who must," Ina wrote in part of her poem. "For those we never give up on, and for those who don't get a chance."[7]

We don't have to go to Third World countries to find big-eyed children who need our help. Poverty-stricken inner city children need us and so does another forgotten population of children— the children of prisoners.

I was in the middle of a book signing session at a small Christian bookstore in Canon City, Colorado, when an older man came into the store with a cute toddler, about eighteen months old, on his shoulders. "Oh, you're having a Saturday with your grandpa!" I said to the child by way of making conversation.

"The easiest thing for me to say would be yes," the man replied, "but actually he's not my grandson. His mother's in prison at one of the state prisons up the road, and he's lived with us since he was three weeks old."

Talking to this godly man, I learned that he and his wife had founded a non-profit ministry that is presently caring for eight children whose mothers are in prison. They take the children to visit their moms on visiting days, unless the moms are in solitary confinement and can't have visitors. Then when the mothers get out, these volunteers work with the system to help the moms get reacquainted with their children and into parenting again. If the mothers decide that they are unable to parent, then the man and his wife are ready and willing to adopt.

In homes with open doors children learn that life is more than making sure our own families are comfortable and have what they need. Sometimes it means sleeping two to a bed so grandma can come visit, or having a whole family move in when they are suddenly without housing due to natural or financial disaster.

"For I was hungry and you gave me something to eat, I was thirsty and you gave me something to drink, I was a stranger and you invited me in, I needed clothes and you clothed me, I was sick and you looked after me, I was in prison and you came to visit me," Jesus said to his disciples (Matt. 25:35-36).

The disciples didn't remember doing all these things for Jesus, so they questioned him about what He said. Jesus explained, "I tell you the truth, whatever you did for one of the least of these brothers of mine, you did for me" (Matt. 25:40).

And whatever we do for the elderly must be especially pleasing to Jesus. My mom was as gracious about living in the same house with my grandmother, her mother-in-law, for the first twenty-five years of her married life as she is to her renters today. Having

Granny there was wonderful for my sisters and me. It meant we never needed a baby-sitter and we always had a friend. Now that families are so transient, and assisted-living facilities are more readily available to a broader segment of the aging population, the benefits of having several generations under one roof are almost forgotten.

Of all the prejudices we need to steer our children away from, one of the closest to home is prejudice against the aging. We all hope to have the privilege of being old some day. Don't we want our children to think kindly of us and treat us humanely when they are the generation in control?

Of course, the primary reason for establishing intergenerational relationships is so the old and the young don't miss the gifts of perspective, wisdom, and shared experiences. It's often said that the older and younger generations have far more in common than either of them has with the generation in between. Grandparents may not understand their adult kids, and kids may not understand their parents, but grandparents and grandkids connect.

If you don't have grandparents nearby, a wonderful way to expose children to the wisdom and friendship of the elderly is to encourage them to participate in a "grandfriends" program at school where older people come in to read and help with lessons. Invite elderly neighbors in for coffee, or take them along to school plays and concerts so they can get to know your children as something other than pests who make noise outside and run through their flowerbeds. All this is part of creating a home with open doors.

The Hospitable Home

One of the reasons the house we live in now feels so much like home is because of the history it has. Not a history based on our eleven years here or the house's longevity in the neighborhood. But a history made up of all the faces that have been around our dining room table. The families and kids who have slept in the bedrooms, or on the floor and couches. The Bible study groups that have gathered and prayed in the living room. In a home with open doors, there is an attitude of welcome, an attitude of hospitality that goes a long way toward making a house a home.

Hospitality is not limited to the Martha Stewart style of entertaining or Julia Child's cuisine. Rather, we extend hospitality to others when we succeed in making them feel comfortable in our presence—whatever it takes. In that regard, we can all be more hospitable to those the world drops on our doorsteps. We don't have to wait until the carpet is clean or we get matching flatware to have neighbors over for dinner. A home with open doors may be a bit dirtier than others. It may be loud at times when neighborhood children or teenagers gather, but it will never be boring or stifling.

"A house empty of children and friends is as useless and forlorn as a railroad station on an abandoned line," reads an anonymous quote. That can never be said of a home with open doors.

"Do not forget to entertain strangers," says Hebrews 13:2, "for by so doing some people have entertained angels without knowing it."

If I've entertained angels, chances are it's been in the kitchen. They probably stood at the counter while I chopped the last of the vegetables for the salad or ground the beans for the coffee. Remember the old saying, "No matter where I serve my guests, they seem to like my kitchen best?" That's so true.

Why do you think people tend to congregate in the kitchen? I've found no amount of coaxing nor delectable hors d'oeuvres can lure my guests into the living room, which I did clean, and out of the kitchen, which is probably a mess.

I think it goes back to that definition of hospitality being our ability to make people feel comfortable. People feel comfortable in the kitchen. They feel even more comfortable if we give them a task to do while we chat with them. Something about the kitchen says, "Come on in. You're family." And nothing is more comfortable than that.

"To be happy at home is the ultimate result of all ambition," Samuel Johnson wrote. I honestly can't think of any way for our families to be happier at home than to make ours homes with open doors. Studies of depression have shown again and again that one of the best ways to beat the blues is to do something for someone else. Likewise, the best way for families to lift their own spirits is to fill the house with guests from time to time. Then maybe we won't worry so much about the leaky gutters or that chugging noise in the furnace. If the house is full of laughter and prayer, you can't hear the drips and the chugs.

Writing this chapter has been very convicting. I'm grateful for growing up in a home with open doors. But I now realize there's so much we could do to open our doors wider.

My husband and I need to join Food for Thought, even if we do have to wear the evangelical Christian label—or maybe because we are privileged to wear it. We need to take more seriously our responsibility to share our Christian worldview with the world around us. Not because it's important for us to be right, but because the truth of salvation is for all people, and Jesus wants them to know it. We need to do it because we live in a world of pain and tragedy that hungers for the simple truths of Creation, the Fall, and the redemption that are at the heart of the Christian worldview.

I want to see more faces of color around my dining room table, and I want the beds that stand empty when the kids and grandkids aren't visiting to be filled more often with people needing a place to stay for a day, or two, or longer.

The wider we open the doors to our homes and to our minds, the more likely it is that we will be able to raise children with a global worldview, compassion for others, and without racial or socioeconomic prejudice. The more we make it possible for them to befriend elderly people or people with disabilities, the more they will embrace the precious gift of life in all its forms. We have to open the doors to let the stagnant air out—and the fragrance of Christ in.

♡ Home Builders:

1. What kind of activities can you use to spark your children's curiosity about different cultures and peoples?
2. Make it a point to reach out to elderly people and those with disabilities. If you don't know any, visit the lonely in nursing homes and hospitals.
3. As followers of Jesus Christ, we should be comfortable with people wearing many different "labels." Are you? Why or why not? What does the word diversity mean to you?

A Home with Memories

●●●●●●●●●●●●●●●

There's no disappointment in memory, and one's
exaggerations are always on the good side.

—George Eliot

For the blessed among us, memories of home are gracious,
comforting ones. They are also selective. We remember
the big overstuffed chair in the living room where we
would snuggle in next to our mom while she read to us, but not
the drafty windows and leaky faucets.

It interests me that whenever I ask very elderly people to share
memories of their past, they almost always skip right over memories of their adult lives, their careers, and even of the families they
raised. Instead, they begin telling me in minute detail about the
kitchen in the home where they grew up. They remember canning
peach preserves or bringing in wood to stoke the wood-burning
stove. They remember home.

What will today's children remember of the homes in which
they are growing up? Are we as parents and grandparents about
the business of making memories, or just about the business of

getting through each day as it comes?

My younger sister, Mary, the mother of three boys, has always been very intentional about making family memories. "Let's make a memory!" she'll declare when she gets an idea for a family outing or project. Her boys might roll their eyes, or even wonder how they might get out of this particular memory-making experience, but Mary's persistence over the years truly has created many wonderful memories for her family. "We have a need as a family to make memories that we can carry into the next generation," she says.

That Mary takes seriously her role as memory maker is a natural extension of the fact that she takes her role as life giver seriously. Women are life givers beyond bringing babies into the world. They are life givers in that they add the qualities to life that raise us all above mere existence. Those things Barbara Mouser, author of *Five Aspects of Woman,* labels "animation, vitality, interest, vigor, and joy." Physically, socially, intellectually, artistically, and spiritually, women are life givers when they create homes where memories can be made and cherished.

Perhaps no generation of life givers deserves more of our respect and admiration than the women who left behind most everything they owned, packed a few keepsakes into the back of a covered wagon, and headed west with their husband and families. Like generations of women before them in civilizations all over the world, they were risking everything they knew and loved to bring life to a new place.

The men who rushed to the West seeking gold or adventure may have set up camps and cleared trails, but it wasn't until women arrived that the West saw the development of towns with schools, churches, libraries, and general stores. The women raised the quality of life above mere survival. Like all women everywhere, they brought forth life and nurtured it spiritually into the next generation.

And it wasn't an easy task. Lillian Schlissel, Director of American Studies at Brooklyn College, studied the diaries of women who were among the quarter of a million Americans who crossed the continental United States between 1840 and 1870. The result was her book *Women's Diaries of the Westward Journey*.

"For while it is true that family history cannot be reconstructed from women's writings alone," Schlissel writes, "nevertheless the women were the shapers of the family, and it is they who provide us with primary access to the internal dynamics of households."[1]

The stories they tell in their diaries are chilling. Not only were the wagons often mired in mud, with all occupants soaked to the bone, but supplies ran short and disease ran rampant. Every diary seems to contain at least one account of a child stricken with dysentery being buried by the side of the road.

The wagons would barely stop long enough for a baby to be born before mother and baby were expected to continue on. While the women's skirts might be torn and caked with mud, they refused to discard them for the more practical bloomers. Why? Because they used them to curtain one another so some modicum of privacy could be observed. Dealing with personal hygiene and menstruation on the open trail was no easy task for these women.

Elizabeth Smith Geer, who started out from Indiana for Oregon Territory with her husband and seven children in the summer of 1847, tells one of the most desperate stories recorded in the overland diaries. During the summer months, the trip went fairly well, but when they reached Oregon in late October, and began to cross the Deschutes River, it was a different picture.

"It rains and snows. We start this morning around the falls with our wagons. . . . I carry my babe and lead, or rather carry, another through snow, mud and water, almost to my knees," Geer wrote. "It is the worst road. . . . I went ahead with my children and I was afraid to look behind me for fear of seeing the

– It Takes a HOME –

wagons turn over in to the mud. . . . I was so cold and numb I could not tell by feeling that I had any feet at all. . . . There was not one dry thread on any of us—not even my babe. . . . I have not told you half we suffered. I am not adequate to the task."[2]

That we owe today's civilized, cultured cities of the West to women like Elizabeth Smith Geer is an understatement. For since Adam renamed woman Eve, meaning life, women have been the life givers in the world. And in their life giving, they have created homes with memories.

Even women who have dedicated most of their adult lives to public and professional achievement find it hard to totally turn away from the life-giving role that provides so much soul satisfaction.

The highly visible news correspondent Cokie Roberts, writing in her book *We Are Our Mothers' Daughters,* says, "I'm always struck by the similarity in women's stories, no matter how different they may superficially seem. That's because of the thread of continuity with women throughout the ages, the sense that we are doing what women have always done even as we pioneer our way across cultural divides or declare a revolution."[3]

When Roberts visited a museum in Greece, she saw displays of ancient needles, buttons, pots, jewelry, and toys. "Here the objects from the everyday lives of women from thousands of years ago overwhelmed me with their familiarity," she writes. "I could have opened the cases, put on their jewels, and taken up their tools, picked up where they left off without a moment's hesitation or confusion."[4]

While Roberts maintains a woman's place is everywhere she wants to be, she also stresses that caretaking and nurturing are always a part of a woman's life—even if they are manifested in an office setting.

These bonds that tie women of all career choices together are the ones we cling to the most. It's in our similarities, not our differences, that we find the mutual support and strength we need to

– 164 –

get our wagons through today's mud. Making memories for our families is important to all women, regardless of career choice. Cookie exchanges, baby-sitting co-ops, and Creative Memories photo album sessions are evidence of our willingness to share our skills and creativity so that we can all reach the ultimate memory-making goal.

Holiday Traditions

And what season is more perfect for making memories than the holiday season? The traditions that evolve from the baking, decorating, and celebrating follow a family from house to house and find a permanent home in the heart of each family member.

I'll never forget the church Advent supper my two boys and I attended when I was a single mom. We made an Advent wreath together and then we were told to join other families in a circle to share our favorite Christmas memories. The divorce was fairly recent, and I was afraid this was going to be pretty hard on all of us emotionally, but there was nothing to do but pull our chairs into the circle and join in.

"As we go around the circle," the group leader explained, "each person will share a favorite Christmas memory." I held my breath when it was my eleven-year-old son Rob's turn. There were still so many positive things to remember about our life as a family. Surely he could think of one. Would he tell about the time we got together with neighbors and made Christmas ornaments, then went caroling? Or maybe he'd talk about cutting out sugar cookies in Christmas shapes, or making snowmen out of popcorn balls.

"The only Christmas I remember is the one when I threw up on my new cowboy outfit," he volunteered.

The second time around the circle, I just knew he'd think of some cherished family tradition to mention. "Is there anything else you remember?" the group leader asked.

"Well, I threw up on the boots too!" he replied.

It's interesting how the negative memories tend to blend in with the positive ones.

Ever since she became a grandmother, my mom's been called Nana, so on Christmas Eve she becomes Nana Claus. Dressed in an old red coat and a well-worn Santa mask and beard, Nana Claus hands out gifts to each person present. All the while she reads a rhymed narrative that she wrote incorporating family happenings, current events, and popular song lyrics.

Even though I haven't been in Tennessee for Christmas in many years, my mother, now eighty-four, continues creating memories for our family, and I notice my sisters and I emulating her in so many ways. I really prefer to visit Tennessee in the springtime when the dogwood is in full bloom, so by choice I don't go home in December. Still, every year I have at least one good cry the first time I play Amy Grant's song, "A Tender Tennessee Christmas."

All the memories my mother created, and continues to create, inspire that annual yearning for home in my heart. Yet, memory-making holiday traditions are as varied and innovative as the families that create them.

One of the saddest aspects of divorce is that traditions get lost along with family history. Ornaments and stockings are divided between homes, and children are torn between families. Even now, with all our children married, the holidays can cause tension if we try too hard to create a "traditional Christmas" in our non-traditional, blended family. Where traditions are concerned, we've learned to be flexible.

So we've learned to be flexible. Rather than stick to strict "turns" as we did when the children were younger, we've encouraged our married children to begin creating traditions of their own. We've found that staying home is the best idea, because sooner or later someone may decide to come spend Christmas with us after all, or drop by for a few days between Christmas and New Year's.

My older sister, Patty, solved the problem of her son's family being torn between sets of parents on Christmas day by creating a new tradition. The Sunday before Christmas is the day everyone gathers at her house to celebrate and open gifts. It's much more fun and relaxing that way.

Decorating the house for each season is certainly one of the life-giving, memory-making traditions my sisters and I inherited from our mother. I decorate whether we're going to have a house full or just the two of us on Christmas morning. We string lights and garlands outside. My snow globe collection goes on the kitchen counter. The ceramic crèche scene I made in 1970 when I was a young Army wife pregnant with my first child goes on its usual shelf in the living room. Along with the sugar cookies, fudge, hot apple cider, and eggnog, these are the traditions our kids and grandkids know they can depend on whenever they come.

There's nothing unique about my decorating. You probably do the same and more. What matters is not how elaborately we decorate, but that in creating a holiday home we show our families we care—and that's a message they can't receive too often.

Of course, making memories has more to do with the time we spend together than anything else. The caution about family traditions is that we not let the traditions become more important than the family they are created for. If mom is too frazzled to read Christmas stories at bedtime because she's busy making traditions happen, then she's too busy.

You may notice I didn't mention Santa Claus. That's because he is conspicuously absent in our Christmas decorations. I don't have a problem with the jolly old elf as long as we teach the kids that his willingness to give to others is the real gift he brings to the world. I just feel that his image is ubiquitous enough at the mall and on television. In our home, I'd rather the focus be on the real "main character" of Christmas, Jesus Christ.

Author Kendra Smiley said she never taught her children to believe in Santa Claus or the Easter Bunny for much the same reason. "I was afraid that when they found out we lied to them about those two, they would wonder if what we were teaching them about Jesus was true!" Kendra said. Instead, gifts are delivered on these occasions by the "Fat Fairy," a funny (but not fitting) name Kendra inherited from her mother. The kids all know the "Fat Fairy" is really their mom!

It's a good idea when your children are still relatively young to ask them what Christmas traditions they remember and cherish, and then forget about everything else. Use the time you reclaim to just sit in front of the tree with the kids for a whole evening. Ask each child which is his or her favorite ornament and why. Pop some popcorn! Get out the sleeping bags and let everyone fall asleep in the glow of the tree lights.

When it comes to Christmas, simple really is best. After all, that first Christmas in Bethlehem was extremely simple, but it's still the only perfect Christmas ever. The more we keep it in mind when we develop our own Christmas traditions, the more precious our memories will be.

Other holidays are perfect for filling a home with memories too. With each year that passes I become more and more fond of Thanksgiving. Uncomplicated by the excessive decorating and gift giving that we seem compelled to do at Christmastime, Thanksgiving is simpler. It's a time for focusing not on what we don't have, but on what we do.

For many years we've observed a tradition that is now a special part of Thanksgivings in our family. After the table is set for Thanksgiving dinner, I put a single kernel of corn at each place (popcorn works just fine). Once everyone is seated, I pass a small bowl or cup from person to person. In turn, each drops his or her kernel of corn into the bowl and says what he or she is most thankful for that year. (I always leave the gravy on the stove and foil on the sweet-potato-and-marshmallow casserole . . . this can take awhile!) This simple sharing bonds young and old, and both laughter and tears are pretty much guaranteed! So are the memories.

After the sharing, when the tears and laughter have subsided, we join hands and say grace. This past year, when I went in the kitchen to fill the gravy boat after all the thanks and the grace had been said, I felt my granddaughter Amanda tugging on my skirt.

"Grancy," she said, almost in tears. "I forgot to say I was thankful for my sister, and for Jesus." She had been the first to drop her corn in the bowl and probably hadn't had time to think of anything more specific than school and family.

"Well, it's not too late, honey," I said. "Come back in the dining room with me." Once I got everyone's attention, Amanda told them the other things she was thankful for, then happily returned to her place to enjoy her turkey and stuffing.

Everyone loves Valentine's Day, but it can be an extra-special time for fathers and daughters. I always got a valentine from my dad—one with lots of fuzzy flocking. When I was living in the dorm at college, and even after I was married, he would still send me these sentimental "To My Daughter" valentines. I smile when I see my husband doing the same for his daughters.

Then there's Easter! Easter brings bunnies everywhere at my house because I raised rabbits as a girl and I just can't get enough of them. It's a time for dying eggs and hiding them in the backyard, but it's also a time when the good news of the Resurrection is openly discussed and God is praised!

Talking about the true meaning of Christian holidays at home definitely has an impact on children. One year the local newspaper interviewed kindergartners in the small town where our oldest granddaughters live. "What does Easter mean to you?" the interviewer asked. Below each of five precious photos in the newspaper were the children's answers. "Bunnies," said one. "Jelly beans," said another, but under my granddaughter Francesca's photo were two simple words: "The cross."

It's impossible for the world to succeed in secularizing Christian holidays and traditions as long as we can keep our focus on the Lord at home.

So what do we do with Halloween? It began as All Saints' Eve, an event on the church calendar, but now has come to include gang rituals and cat sacrifices. Over the years, I became very concerned about participating in this holiday. After all, doesn't Satan prowl the world every day of the year? Why set aside a special day in honor of evil?

In what may have been an over-reaction, I gave out Scripture verses along with the candy in an attempt to save the little souls that showed up at our door from the Evil One. My husband and I volunteered to help at our church's harvest festival, an alternative to Halloween trick-or-treating.

I still support alternative activities, especially because they are safer than trick-or-treating door-to-door, but I no longer get overly concerned about our grandchildren celebrating Halloween. After all, I can so clearly remember how much my son Tim loved this holiday. He used to try to decide which was his favorite holiday, Halloween or Christmas. I assured him he could just enjoy both, but he seemed obsessed with deciding which was his favorite.

Today he is a Presbyterian minister, so obviously his spiritual life wasn't permanently damaged by the fact that he dressed up as The Fonz from "Happy Days" and went door to door collecting candy. When I hear young Christian moms today wondering how to approach Halloween, I encourage them to let their kids participate, but to focus on the fun characters and images, not the scary ones. After all, it's a good time of year to connect with neighbors and friends—to be candy corn in the world as well as salt and light! And it's a great opportunity to take memory-building photographs.

Year-round Memory Making

Often it's the year-round family traditions that mean the most. Unique family traditions say, "There's no family just like mine, and I'm glad I belong here." These traditions go far toward establishing a family's character and heritage, and to filling a home with memories.

My stepdaughter Julie and her husband, Ryan, have established a heartwarming good-night routine with their toddler twin girls. Every night when it's time for bed, Julie and Ryan take Morgan and Riley into the hallway to say good-night to all their grandmas and grandpas pictured in photos there. Not only does this help the girls remember us between visits, it also helps them wind down from the day and get ready to go to sleep.

An octogenarian friend of mine, Myrtle, continues a tradition today that she started when her two girls were not much older than Julie and Ryan's. She keeps a guest book in the front hall of her home, and everyone who enters the house for a visit "signs in." Once a year, all the names are put in a hat, one name is drawn, and the winner gets a prize!

"I don't decide on the prize until I see who wins," Myrtle said. "That way I can choose something appropriate." Even though Myrtle's grown daughters may or may not be present for the drawing, they always call to see who won! When they were little, it was their job to make sure each guest signed the guest book, and the contest tradition increased their interest in all the people the family entertained.

At the big farmhouse that is headquarters for Jill Savage's family and ministry, Hearts at Home, birthdays are a big occasion. "The night before someone's birthday, while the birthday person is sleeping, we sneak in and decorate his or her room with streamers and balloons," she said. "And we always have ice cream and cake for breakfast to celebrate each birthday!"

Another family brings a unique twist to everyday breakfasts.

"My husband is sort of a short-order cook at breakfast time, and it just works out best if everyone eats the eggs or pancakes as soon as they are ready," the mom explained. "So at breakfast, instead of saying grace before we eat, we say a prayer together at the end of the meal. It's a great way to start the day."

A big part of the memory building in our family has always been the taking and sharing of photos. In case of fire, I always planned to save my photo albums and the file containing our birth certificates. However, I just counted my photo albums, and if you include the grandma brag books, wedding albums, and baby books, I have seventy-six of them. I better hope for a slow-moving fire.

In every family there's always one person who pulls out a camera and says, "OK, everybody, look this way." I have to confess that in our family, that person is me. I think I got it from my dad. He loved to take pictures, especially of the flagpoles at the historic sites we visited on vacation. Of course, to get the flagpole in the photo, he'd have to stand across the street. We have a lot of pictures of flagpoles with my sisters and me huddled around the bottom looking like waving ants.

Now digital cameras are all the rage. It's fun to get up-to-date grandchild photos over the web, but I don't want those grainy printouts to replace photos I can put in albums. (Just as I hate to see e-mail replacing real letters. It's nice to get an e-mail, but it just isn't the same kind of keepsake.)

We also have many rolls of video film that (as my husband is quick to point out) we never look at. But we might someday! I treasure a video I took of my mom sharing memories of her childhood and her courtship with my dad. Until I did that video, I didn't know she first spotted him selling popcorn at a University of Tennessee football game. No wonder she's still such a big fan!

All the photography and videotaping is just my way of saying, "This is a precious moment, and I want to hold on to it a little longer." Moms and grandmas are just like that, I guess.

Family vacations are perfect memory-building experiences, and everyone appreciates home even more when they've been away from it for awhile. My most memorable childhood vacation was our great trek west in 1960. Although most of the trip went relatively smoothly, it's the misadventure we all remember most. Somewhere in Nevada, our tuned-to-Tennessee automobile overheated. My dad carried jugs of extra water to cool down the radiator, and while he and my mom were outside pouring the water on it and watching the steam rise, my older sister and I were cruelly teasing our younger sister, Mary, who was eight.

As far as we could see in every direction from the windows of our '59 Chevy station wagon, there was nothing but cactus and dust. Patty and I told Mary that our family was going to be stranded there forever, and that all we had to eat was the tiny box of raisins in the glove compartment. To this day, my little sister experiences a wave of anxiety whenever she sees a box of Sunmaid raisins, but we all still laugh about it after forty years!

Another memory-making vacation was the one on which my husband and I took our blended family a few years after we married. We chose a houseboat excursion to Lake Powell, believing that the only way we would get our teenagers to relate to one another and to us was to take them completely away from malls, telephones, friends, and significant others.

Our strategy worked beautifully, but it isn't the memory of the emerald green waters, the Anasazi ruins, or the nights under the starry skies that we all mention first when we talk about the vacation. It's the day a storm came up unexpectedly and the winds tossed our boat, uprooted our shoreline anchors, and blew the mattresses from the roof of the houseboat into the water. Quickly we became a well-tuned crew, and soon everything was secured. We had survived the storm, and we had bonded in the process. That's what we remember when we look at those photos.

No matter how hard we try to create wonderful memories for our families, however, what people remember most fondly are the spontaneous moments. When my boys talk about their growing-up years, they say things like, "Remember when we tied sheets around our shoulders and jumped off the deck thinking we could fly like super heroes?" It's these shared, unscripted moments that create the warmest memories.

That's why it's so important to create a home where people can be themselves and things flows naturally. "Home is where life makes up its mind," reads one popular motto. And the physical surroundings aren't nearly as important as the human interactions taking place inside the walls of that place called home.

When I asked my sister Mary for her thoughts on home, she said, "When we built our new home, we were able to add more rooms than we had in our old house, but we still use the kitchen the most. This is the room where breakfast is eaten from bar stools, where homework is done at the last minute, where the laundry is folded as we talk over the day, where the news is watched and popcorn is popped nightly, where meals are prepared in the midst of activities, and where last-minute bills are paid. It's where clothes are ironed on the table, where the cat looks through the window when he wants inside, where the refrigerator is checked for something new several times an hour. It's here that schoolwork or honors are displayed, and guests hang out regardless of the size of the party. It's where the trash is gathered and gathered, where prayers are said, where we greet one another after a long day, where flowers are arranged, where school projects are created, and where everyone feels loved and at home. My only question is, why didn't we just build a house that was all kitchen?"

Most of our memories of home seem to center around the kitchen, maybe because food is such a big part of what we remember too. Domesticity as an art form came under attack by certain factions of the feminist movement, but it's wonderfully satisfying to create delicious, nourishing meals and maintain a home that is both comforting and inviting. Now, Baby Boomers are rediscovering the value of "nesting" and "cocooning." Home decorating, gardening, and cooking enterprises are focusing more attention on the domestic arts.

"The woman who sustains and creates a home, and under whose hands children grow up to be strong and pure men and women is a creator second only to God," wrote American author Helen Hunt Jackson in the mid-nineteenth century. That's a mighty high compliment, and hard to keep in mind as we are engaged in the more grueling, thankless tasks of housekeeping. But it's true that we can still take pleasure from domestic chores when we consider that we are not just chopping carrots or dusting bookshelves; we're creating a home where memories will be made.

Housekeeping, Homemaking, and Housebuilding

Barbara Mouser, in her *Five Aspects of Woman* Bible study, differentiates between housekeeping, homemaking, and housebuilding, but sees them all as opportunities for women to use and develop skills designed for higher purposes.

Mouser reminds us that although the physical upkeep of the home, housekeeping, can be frustrating; it can also rest the mind from intense intellectual labors and relieve the soul of larger-than-life stresses. Although I don't mind having help when I can get it, I always feel more in touch with my home when I clean it myself. In fact, I can't imagine any woman feeling totally at home in a new location until she's gotten down on her hands and knees on the kitchen floor.

By contrast, homemaking, Mouser states, "is habitually creating an atmosphere at home conducive to rest, fellowship, love, learning and security."[5] It is a feminine art form for all women, and includes all the things that my husband is quick to admit, "need a woman's touch."

"The wise woman builds her house, but with her own hands the foolish one tears hers down." Proverbs 14:1 says. Mouser writes:

Housebuilding, in this sense, can be defined as the long-term life work of helping a man, creating and nurturing a family, producing wealth, earning a reputation, blessing the local church and the community, strengthening the nation, and thus influencing the world.

Housework is not the same thing as homemaking, and homemaking is not the same thing as housebuilding. Understanding these three different aspects of your relationship to the inner domain of the home will help you guard your priorities, maintain your self-respect, and keep your long-term focus. If a woman thinks she is only a toilet-bowl washer, it is little wonder she would feel angry and underemployed. On the other hand, if she organizes her life in order to build a family who will have an impact on the world, she will have little trouble with confidence or purpose. The highest does not stand without the lowest. It is necessary to keep a house in order to make a home and build a family. The mundane and the majestic are both part of the homemaking career.[6]

When I worked full time I used to yearn for days at home. I wanted to make myself a cup of tea in the middle of the morning and sit and watch the cats sleeping in the sunbeams stretched across the wood floor. When I decided to quit my job to work at home, I looked forward to having time to organize all my closets and cupboards and to simply get in touch with my home again.

I did all that, and it felt as good as everyone working full time imagines it would. Cupboards don't stay organized and cats don't always nap in the sunlight, but taking a day off every so often to be an at-home mom or homemaker can be immensely satisfying, not to mention sanity saving. To deny the yearning we have as women to create nests for our families and ourselves is to deny a beautiful part of God's created purpose for us—not the only part, but a beautiful part.

It's in those nests where memories are made, and that same nesting instinct moves from our homes, cluttered or well-organized, into the world in which our families work, play, and grow.

"I have noticed as I raised my boys that when we were all together as a family in a close place, I would have an overwhelming sense of peace, contentment, and warmth," my sister Mary wrote. "These close places could be a booth at a restaurant, our family car, or the couch in our den, but my very favorite 'close place' is our church pew when it is crowded and we have to snuggle together to fit in. One Christmas Eve we were late to the service and the ushers led us to the front row where we had to wrap our arms around each other to fit. When the sermon began and the Advent candles were lit, I knew this was the closest to heaven I had ever come. Maybe there is something to this mother hen stuff and gathering in the chicks. It's the yearning for the contentment and peace that comes from having your family close to you."

Having family close—even if they are only close in heart and memory—is what makes a house a home. Not all the memory making you do will be remembered, but some of it will. And like Mary, the mother of Jesus, you can keep all these things and ponder them in your heart.

♡ Home Builders:

1. What traditions did your family observe when you were growing up? Which of those traditions have you carried forward into your own home?
2. Have you ever considered the difference between housekeeping, homemaking, and housebuilding? Which needs more of your attention?
3. What are your fondest and most vivid memories from childhood? Why do you think those memories have stayed with you?

A Home in a Village

• • • • • • • • • • • • • •

One thing I know: The only ones among you who
will be really happy are those who will have sought
and found how to serve.

—*Albert Schweitzer*

The premise behind this entire book is that the home is
more critical than the village to the welfare and education of the child. Still, it would be foolish to deny that the
home is in a village in the sense that we live in communities,
towns, and states. The home also has a responsibility to the village, and the people in the home must be willing to leave home
to go into the community to work at making it better—and to
serve others.

As in all aspects of their acculturation, children learn best about
being good citizens by watching what their parents do. Do parents
vote? Do they volunteer their time and resources to community
organizations and churches? If so, then the children will also.

The home is the encampment from which people go out to
change and affect their communities. Of course there are exceptions, but the political position that the community must move into

every home in order for the children to be raised effectively is simply not so. The role of parents in the home is still far more critical than any role the village, with its government programs and policies, can begin to play. Do such programs have a purpose in saving those without the resources and protection a home provides? Of course. The concern I have is that existing homes sometimes fail to accept the responsibility that is primarily theirs.

Our understanding of the role of the family and the importance of the home should always begin with biblical basics. God created Eve for Adam, and they became "one flesh," establishing the unity in marriage of a man and a woman. The seventh commandment, "Thou shalt not commit adultery," certainly endorses monogamous marriage as God's perfect plan. The command in Genesis 1:28 to "Be fruitful and increase in number; fill the earth and subdue it" establishes God's plan for families and their role in the world.

After reviewing these biblical basics, Charles M. Sell, the author of a classical seminary text titled *Family Ministry,* goes on to say: "That ideally children are to be raised by their parents and not by the extended family, tribe, or community seems clear by the fact that one of the ten commandments was for children to honor their parents (Ex. 20:12). Parents were commanded to teach their children about God (Deut. 6:7). Though the word 'parents' is not actually used, it seems clear that the teaching is to be done at home: 'Talk about them when you sit at home and when you walk along the road, when you lie down and when you get up'" (Deut. 6:7). [1]

God is for families and with parents. He wants families to survive, in spite of all the cultural evidence to the contrary, and He will intervene to reinforce the hearts and guide the decisions of obedient, willing parents.

When drugs, immorality, and gun violence invade our schools and neighborhoods, our first impulse may be to keep our families sheltered within the physical walls of the home, limiting the exposure of each precious member to all the dangers and evil in the world. But especially as Christian parents, we just don't have that luxury. We are to live in the world until we are called out of it, and living in the world means being willing to venture outside the walls of home to have a positive influence on those around us.

"Whether your family is large or small, whether your resources are sparse or extensive, every Christian parent is called to make the home a ministry," wrote Chuck Colson. "That means educating our children in a biblical worldview and equipping them to have an impact on the world. In the long run, this is the best way that Christians can restore and redeem the surrounding culture."[2]

In order to have effective ministries, families must be well informed about community issues that could affect their health, their economic well being, and the education of their children. Every home in the village should be aware of environmental concerns, for instance. Parents and children can work together to recycle, pick up litter, or whatever is necessary to positively manage the environment as they follow God's mandate to rule the world. They do this to be good citizens of the village, although ultimately, they—not the village—are accountable to God for taking care of His world.

Recycling is one of the easiest ways to get even the youngest children aware of the world around them and their responsibility to it. A family recycling center in the garage makes it easy for toddlers to deposit aluminum cans and plastic bottles in the designated bags for delivery to a recycling center. Children notice when parents see litter at the park or on the playground and take the time to pick it up and put it in the nearest trash receptacle. Lessons about taking care of God's world are as simple as that. And unfortunately, there's enough discarded trash to make this lesson easy to repeat most any time.

Volunteer Power

Once children learn to care about the world around them in such small, basic ways, they are able to open their hearts and minds to projects with even more impact. In chapter nine we explored the benefits of living in a home with open doors so that children learn to reach out to others. This is part of their responsibility as citizens of the community.

One Thanksgiving I was surprised to see my neighbor Barbara and her daughter Annie, twelve, on the evening news. They were standing in a line with other volunteers scooping out mashed potatoes and gravy to the homeless people being served by the Salvation Army that day. When I asked Barbara and Annie why they decided to volunteer, their responses were heartwarming.

"When you stop to think about it, we all have so much," Barbara said. "I thought this would be one way our family could give back to the community. Besides, I thought it would be fun for Annie and I to do it together!"

"It was a cool thing to do!" Annie said. "I liked serving the food and helping those people."

When kids see parents volunteering, they want to volunteer too. In a survey commissioned by Prudential, 95 percent of the teenagers polled said they supported volunteering. Almost two-thirds said that individual responsibility is the best way to solve community problems, and 67 percent indicated that they devote some of their time to volunteer activities.[3]

Why do kids volunteer? In addition to wanting to make a difference in the community or world, they volunteer because it helps them develop new skills, explore career paths, and because they have fun working with friends. All together, volunteering makes kids feel good about themselves, and increasing self-esteem is critical to keeping kids out of trouble and involved in productive activities.

Wise parents encourage kids to follow their passions when

deciding where and how to volunteer. Do they enjoy reading? Encourage them to tutor younger readers or work at a literacy center teaching adults or children. Is being outdoors their passion? Then suggest volunteering for a parks program to rebuild trails or construct playgrounds. Have a sports fanatic in your family? Many sports organizations for youth love to have teenagers volunteer to work with the coaches and kids. All the experience these volunteer teens get goes far in helping them develop the work ethic and sense of responsibility that will increase their likelihood of success in a paid position later.

Young children often have a passion for animals. Caring for our furry friends is certainly a part of the stewardship we are to have for creation. Even older elementary kids and middle schoolers can volunteer to walk an elderly neighbor's dog or help out in summer programs at local zoos or animal shelters. They may have to begin by shoveling poop and cleaning cages, but that's a lesson volunteers have to learn too: you can't expect to begin at the top!

Often a whole family adopts a cause near and dear to its heart. A coworker of mine was devastated to learn that her two young daughters both have cystic fibrosis. She and her husband, a judge, now devote most of their volunteer time to raising funds and public awareness about this disease.

Both of the girls have been active in the fundraising too. Each year the local Cystic Fibrosis Foundation conducts a direct-mail campaign, and over the years the engaging faces of Samantha and Libby have gone from those of chubby-cheeked toddlers to those of sophisticated teens. Comments from the girls about their hopes for the future are usually part of the appeal for funds to further CF research.

Being a spokesperson for CF is a role Samantha, the older of the two girls, became fairly comfortable with as she grew up. But she then took her passion for volunteering and the experience she gained through participating in CF fundraising to serve on the board of The Juvenile Diabetes Foundation. Why that particular cause? "All through my childhood, my friend Natalie and I were inseparable," Sam said. "She was always there for me. I even remember her breaking open her piggy bank for a fund raiser for cystic fibrosis. So when I learned that she had juvenile diabetes, it was natural for me to get involved in helping her."

Saying it strengthens her to give to others, Sam also volunteers at the Children's Literacy Center and has won award after award for her effective results and dedication to all her volunteer commitments. Now a freshman at the University of Colorado majoring in pre-med, she says volunteering will always be a part of her life.

"My parents are my role models. The way they deal with having two children with cystic fibrosis and the way they give so much back to others has inspired me," Sam said. "I strongly believe that if everyone gives a little bit back, then a web of support and compassion will be formed so that no one will be alone in their time of need."

Another inspiring story concerns a fourth-grade class in Aurora, Colorado, that collectively decided to take a stand on the issue of slavery. The teacher of this class told them about slavery in Africa, including the horrible details about Christian women and children being stolen by Muslim slavers and taken from their homes into northern Sudan. The children were so touched that they began to cry.

"We thought slavery was over," they said.

But they didn't despair without trying to right the situation. Whereas many adults would have accepted the situation as unchangeable, the kids didn't. Instead, they formed a group called Slavery That Oppresses People, or STOP. They learned about the group Christian Solidarity International, a human rights group that redeems slaves by purchasing them and returning them to their families—then they began collecting money. The kids contributed their allowances first, but they also sold lemonade, T-shirts, and old toys. With the addition of donations from corporate donors, they soon had enough money to buy freedom for 150 slaves. That's making a difference.[4]

Volunteering doesn't always feel so rewarding. Sometimes, even when we know we are being used by God in a particular outreach, we wonder why we don't see more visible results for our efforts. Part of what we have to remember, and teach our children, is that God sees what we are doing—and that's all that matters when we are doing it for His glory.

Presently I volunteer to lead a weekly devotion at an assisted living facility populated by a wonderful group of seniors, many in wheelchairs, on walkers, or connected to portable oxygen tanks. Every Tuesday morning I share another of the inspirational writings from the book *Devotional Classics,* edited by Richard J. Foster and James Bryan Smith. I begin by reading the excerpt for the day, along with the accompanying Scripture passage. Then we discuss the questions at the end of the chapter and go over the suggested exercises for the week.

Although I know the Spirit is always present, or I wouldn't have the courage to attempt this at all, some days He seems more involved than other days. On those good days, the discussions are lively and the non sequiturs are few. Residents share precious memories of beloved departed spouses or regale the group with tales of past travels and life experiences. We laugh and cry together on a good day.

But some Tuesday mornings I leave wondering if my being there had any impact at all. One low point was when a dear but confused resident named Rose wandered into the session and took a seat. I continued discussing the topic at hand when she piped up in a very loud voice, "God? Did you say God? Now, there's a subject we wouldn't want to bring up!" I smiled and nodded and kept right on going—after all, it was His devotion time! Volunteering isn't always immediately gratifying, and we need to help our children understand that.

One of the things my husband and I do to encourage our adult, married kids to reach out to others is our "Christmas Gift Opt-out Program." In any given year, they are encouraged to do something for someone else instead of buying a gift for us. All we ask is that they write us a letter telling about their volunteer projects. One letter told us of experiences at a soup kitchen. Another gave a detailed description of the contents of a shoebox full of gifts sent to a little girl in Bosnia. These letters are among the best gifts we've ever received.

When General Colin Powell retired from the Army, many speculated that he would enter the political arena. Instead, he decided to dedicate himself to promoting volunteer programs for people of all ages and races. As chairperson for a national crusade for young people called America's Promise—The Alliance for Youth, he lists five basic promises to America's youth. Promises that I believe can most effectively be kept by a home in a village, rather than by the village itself. The promises are:

- An ongoing relationship with a caring adult—a parent, mentor, tutor, or coach
- Safe places and structured activities during nonschool hours
- A healthy start
- A marketable skill through effective education
- An opportunity to give back through community service

Offering as an example his own after-school job for a man who ran a toy store in the South Bronx, Powell makes the point that once one of the above promises is kept, two or three others are likely to be kept as well. "I had a safe place to go after school and on weekends; I had a chance to learn marketable skills; and I had a mentor," Powell recalls of his job at fourteen.[5]

Educational Options

Reading down the list of five promises, it's obvious the village can play a role in fulfilling each one of them—but I still believe the home plays the strongest role. Only when it comes to the education of children do I find myself, like many parents and grandparents, in a quandary as to just how much the village should be involved in the fulfillment of the promise.

Perhaps there isn't a definitive answer to the question of which educational choice—public, private, or home schooling—is best for everyone. Parents need to pray and carefully consider their decision based on the needs of each child and the family resources available for education. What we can be sure of is that they must be constantly vigilant and involved in their children's education regardless of the option they choose.

I know my comfort with public education is based primarily on personal experience; I went to public schools and so did my children. There were fewer options available in the '50s and '70s than there are today. But because I believe in raising children in homes with open doors, homes that teach a worldview, I tend to lean in favor of exposing children to a diverse classroom with children of many socio-economic, ethnic, and cultural backgrounds.

I worry that some children may be shortchanged if they aren't allowed to take advantage of the physical facilities and technological resources a public school can provide. More importantly, I worry that in their comparative isolation, they may be prevented from developing the skills they will need as adults to get along with people very different from themselves. Whereas many home schoolers are involved in athletics, I wonder if the team sport experience is the same for them as for the children whose teammates are also classmates.

Yet, in light of liberal curriculum and the absence of moral absolutes in many public schools, I understand why more and

more parents are saying, "We can do a better job." Even before
the most recent rash of school violence episodes, home schooling
was growing, up 7 to 15 percent in the last five years with 1.2 million to 1.6 million children educated at home in 1998, according
to figures from the National Home Education Research Institute. [6]

The benefits of home schooling are many. Parents can make
sure their children learn the Christian beliefs of historical heroes
like Christopher Columbus who credited the Holy Spirit with
directing his journey. They can freely teach the biblical principles
on which the Founding Fathers relied when they drafted the
Declaration of Independence and the Constitution. "The longer I
live," Benjamin Franklin said, "the more convincing proofs I see
of this truth: That God governs in the affairs of men." John Adams
wrote, "Our Constitution was made only for a moral and religious
people. It is wholly inadequate to the government of any other."[7]
Home schooling parents can also pray openly with their children.

Beyond the educational benefits, many home schooling moms
genuinely enjoy their children and want more time with them during the precious years they are at home. Granted, adding teaching
to an already busy schedule of running a home and family can be
a challenge, but they are willing to sacrifice to make it happen,
and so they do.

"My daughter really wanted a year at home with her mama,"
one mom who home schooled her children told me. "I thought I
would be a fool to miss the opportunity. What I found amazingly
rewarding was the relationship building that occurred. Home
schooling is just a wonderful opportunity to invest time in all areas
of your children's lives. I know we are a stronger family for the
experience."

There are times when home schooling works this well—and
times when it doesn't. When it works well is when the parents are
capable of teaching, if not trained to do so. One family in our
community home schools all three of their children, now in

eleventh, ninth, and sixth grades. But the children's mother is a nationally acclaimed educator and author. As if that isn't enough substantiation for home schooling, the children's grandfather lives in the home and participates in their education too. He's a retired minister and directs the religious education of the children every morning. The benefits of such an arrangement are undeniable.

What concerns me, however, is that more and more young mothers, especially Christian moms, are home schooling their children whether or not they have the qualifications or passion to do so because of pressure from peers and churches. That these decisions may be made without taking into consideration the individual educational and socialization needs of the children is equally concerning. The wise home schooling family only commits to one year at a time, and when it's determined that home schooling isn't working, either for the parent-teacher or for a child in the home schooling environment, they don't hesitate to make a change.

It takes many homes in a village working together to support the educational opportunities the village can provide, but this doesn't mean the village must dictate every aspect of education. Debates about school vouchers and tax credits will continue, but regardless of the decisions reached, public schools can and should thrive. Charter schools, definitely on the increase because of their return to the classical disciplines, can and should thrive. Private schools, for those who can afford them, can and should thrive. Home schooling should be supported as a viable option for many. The goal, after all, is to make education stimulating and encouraging to the children we are trying to reach—and reach them we must.

"Ten years ago one pediatrician noted to me that he saw the light go out in the eyes of many fifth and sixth graders," says psychologist and theologian Robert J. Wicks. "Now she sees this same sad shroud over their spontaneity in the second and third grades."[8]

The light goes out when children face too many can'ts and

not enough cans. It goes out when they feel that the adults who matter most in their lives have no time for them—and no interest in them.

It is up to each family to keep the light burning. It is up to each family to assess the needs of the children, the finances, and the social and moral beliefs they aren't willing to sacrifice before the right decision about the education of children can be made. Once it is made, it must be constantly re-evaluated, and the parents must remain involved in all aspects of the educational experience if they want their children to come from a home in the village, not a home controlled by the village.

Author John MacArthur, writing in *Successful Christian Parenting,* cautions parents about being lulled into thinking that the responsibility for the education of the children lies outside the home. After reading *It Takes a Village,* by Hillary Rodham Clinton, he said that he felt the book was primarily written to set forth an agenda that would move America closer to state-sponsored parenting.

MacArthur's primary concern with this direction is based on his observation that "if anything has been made clear over the past half century, it is that biblical values are certainly not deemed acceptable in any government-sponsored program in America." It's his fear that Mrs. Clinton's village would indoctrinate children with secular humanism instead.[9]

I also read Mrs. Clinton's book, and I enjoyed it far more than I thought I would. It is well written and researched, and some statements she makes, such as that "there is no substitute for regular, undivided attention from parents," had me cheering in my chair.[10] The problem is that while the author clearly articulates and examines every major social issue impacting children today, her solutions almost always call for more government intervention, which by default results in less parental responsibility.

"The crux of the issue is whether our schools, community

agencies, churches, business and political processes will foster or destroy family life," Charles M. Sell wrote. "For example, how the federal government supports childcare will either support or shatter families. Providing money solely for day care centers will promote the separation of children from their families. Instead, money could be directed in such a way that parents could benefit from caring for their children at home or at least pay relatives or friends to help them."[11]

The Child Care Dilemma

Certainly no issue is more emotion packed than that of child care. A home in a village maintains the primary responsibility for making the decisions about how the children in that home will be cared for, who needs to work outside the home, and who will be at home, without intervention from the village. We can only pray that these decisions are also made without the bias the materialistic, achievement-oriented society in which we live so readily provides.

Far too many of society's misdirected messages are aimed at mothers. Columnist Kathleen Parker articulated so well what so many of us feel when we hear all the woes of childcare being tossed to the unnamed "they" of society.

"What few seem willing or able to see is that the 'they' is us, and so is the solution. Not government, not a billion-dollar daycare industry, not men. . . . The key words that are unutterably hard to say is we have to manage our own lives—in different, individualized ways."

Parker, who writes her column from home, goes on to add that there is someone to blame in the child care mess in which we find ourselves. She says that they are "the purveyors of half-truths who made women feel that staying home to mother a child was indentured servitude and who made men feel no longer responsible for their families. 'They,' unfortunately, were us," Parker states, "and it's long past time to correct the record."[12]

We can't afford to be so elitist that we don't realize the numbers of single parents living in poverty who need help caring for their children so that the children can be brought up safely and developmentally sound. We can't ignore the fact that many single mothers have no option other than to work full time to keep food on the table and shoes on their kids' feet. Yet neither can we afford to assume that all children need government-run day-care programs in order to thrive. My prayer is that more parents will take all options under consideration before buying into child care outside the home as the only option.

Fortunately, we human parents still possess the intelligence and creativity to come up with positive solutions. Flextime sometimes allows both parents to work part time and share the child-tending responsibilities. Friends and relatives still pitch in, not because they have to but because they want to. And based on the success of car-pooling and play groups, more and more parents are expanding the concept of cooperative child care to include after-school care for children of working couples.

Churches, too, when they are about the business of equipping the members of their congregation and communities to live out biblical truth in the world, are responding to the need by offering classes that encourage and instruct parents. They also offer alternative activities for children and teens, and many open their doors for after-school care.

Sometimes, a home in a village becomes an after-school home for a whole neighborhood. Such was the case when retired couple Conrad and Millie Schapp welcomed two children who were going door-to-door for a school fund-raiser into their home. By the time the kids left, the Schapps had invited them to go to their church and had given them each a Bible.

The next day, three more kids showed up wanting to know if they could have one of those books the other kids got. Now, on any given Wednesday afternoon, as many as fifteen kids ranging in age from preschoolers to teenagers may show up for the Schapps after-school Bible club. Before the afternoon is over, they might have watched a video, had a Bible lesson, or sung some songs. For sure, they will have had one of Millie's hot meals—and a lot of Kool-Aid.

"This is God's setup," says sixty-five-year-old Millie. "He sent the kids here."

Her husband Conrad, sixty-four, agrees.

"Everybody knows neighborhood kids," he says. "If you want God to use you, pray and look for opportunities to respond. Many times opportunity comes knocking at your door."[13]

An astute, actively involved home in a village will hear the knock when it comes. It will also be engaged in promoting programs that solve the biggest problems while being proactive in supporting the role of the family for the sake of the individuals in it. This proactive role may be played out at PTA meetings and on soccer fields, but it must also be played out at the polls if the changes are to be long lasting and far reaching.

A poll commissioned by the Family Research Council asked Americans to rate nine day care options. The option of a child being cared for by his own mother came out on top. Care by other family members, friends, or a nanny were next. Care by a government-run center came out at the bottom.

In reporting these findings, Chuck Colson wrote, "Parents may know something government bureaucrats don't: Full-time care at daycare centers isn't good for kids." Negatives he lists include separation anxieties, aggression, and new strains of serious illnesses that thrive in the day-care environment. Favoring tax credits to parents who raise their kids themselves, Colson urges parents to "let our legislators know that government funding of daycare centers is not the answer. Instead, we need tax policies that will help parents themselves do what parents do best—'to raise up a child in the way he should go.'"[14]

The willingness of parents to give the government and other institutions sole responsibility for raising their children is symptomatic of our society's reticence to accept responsibility for our actions in general. But these are children we're talking about, not jobs or traffic tickets. We need to build more homes with parents dedicated to fulfilling their God-given responsibility to raise their children in the way He would have them grow.

A home in a village learns to reach out to others and to participate in the schools, churches, and community activities the village offers without losing sight of the primary role the home must play. We are not called to be isolationists, but to connect with others.

"Either we can live as unique members of a connected community, experiencing the fruit of Christ's life within us, or we can live as terrified, demanding, self-absorbed islands, disconnected from community and desperately determined to get by with whatever resources we brought to our island with us," wrote Larry Crabb in his book *Connecting*.[15]

Rather than being islands to themselves, homes in a village need to be more like tugboats, traveling wherever they need to go to help, but secure in knowing that in Christ they have all the power they need to do the job.

It takes many such secure, well-functioning homes to create the kind of village in which we all want to live.

Home Builders:

1. What sorts of activities does your family engage in that strengthen both the village and the home?
2. How have you arrived at your decisions about education? What are you doing to ensure your education plan is working well?
3. If you have children in child care, is it time to review your decision? What other options are open to you, if any?

A Home Revisited

· · · · · · · · · · · · · ·

Where we love is home. Home that our feet
may leave but not our hearts.

—*Oliver Wendell Holmes Jr.*

The first trip I made home to Tennessee after my dad died
in 1986 was a difficult one. It was strange to get off the
plane and not find him waiting for me at the airport, his
head towering above all the other expectant people craning their
necks to find the person they came to meet.

Stepping inside the two-story white farmhouse where I had
grown up was difficult too. The old house wasn't the same without my dad there. Yet, it was comforting to know that I could still
come home in a true sense.

This house has been home to me since the day my mom carried me in from the hospital swaddled in pink blankets.
Returning so many years later, it seemed to wrap its arms around
me as it always had, the familiar sights and smells providing a
warm blanket to insulate me from the grief that followed me
wherever I went.

Later in that same visit, I took my camera and went for a walk. I didn't think my mother planned on moving anytime soon, but nothing seemed as certain as it had before my dad died so suddenly of heart failure. I took a photo of the house from several different angles.

Then I walked down to take a photo of the barn where I had kept my horse, Dolly. Dolly was "handed down" to me after my older sister, Patty, discovered make-up and boys. I still think I got the best part of that deal. Every afternoon after school I would throw down my books, change into my jeans, and race down to the barn to ride Dolly.

Framed in my viewfinder was a faded red barn listing dangerously to one side. But what I saw as memory kicked in was a sunlit afternoon when I put the bridle on Dolly, then swung up onto her back to race through the hay fields and up the hill behind my house.

Anyone seeing my assortment of photos from home might wonder why I took one of the driveway leading up to the house. They wouldn't know it wasn't just an ordinary driveway. This was the driveway where I learned to ride a tricycle, then a bike, and finally, where I drove the family station wagon back and forth before I got my driver's license. It's the driveway where I sat in cars talking to dates until my dad blinked the porch light to tell me it was time to come in. People talk about the highways and byways of life, but so much of life is really lived out in the driveways. I wanted a photo of mine.

I even took a photo of the mailbox at the end of the driveway. After all, this was the mailbox that brought college acceptances and love letters from distant beaus. It's the mailbox that collected all my letters home from Germany in the early '70s, with photos of my baby sons tucked inside.

If anything should ever happen to this place I knew as home, I wanted to make sure I had the photos to remember it by. In retrospect, I realize the pictures were totally unnecessary. I might enjoy showing them to a Colorado grandchild someday, but it's impossible for me to ever forget anything about my original birthplace and home. It's a part of me.

It's been fourteen years since that visit, and my eighty-four-year-old mom still lives in the house. My sisters and I have tried to encourage her to simplify her life by downsizing to a smaller home, but she won't budge. When we ask her why she won't consider living some place more manageable, she says, "Because I live here, that's why!" If she wants to stay there, we want to help her do it. But we also want to make sure she understands that she doesn't have to hold on to "the homeplace," as she calls it, for our sake. That home is a part of each one of us; we will always have it with us wherever we go.

A plaque that hangs on my kitchen wall in Colorado is a daily reminder of this truth. "You never really leave a place you love," it reads. "Part of it you take with you, leaving a part of you behind." So it is with home. Especially the childhood homes of our memories.

"Step onto the highway of any man or woman's heart, start walking, and you will eventually arrive back at the home of their childhood," wrote Mary Farrar in her book, *Choices*. [1] It's that yearning to go home again that keeps travel agents busy and airports full over the holidays. Even if the physical structure is nothing like it used to be, and mom and dad have traded in the farmhouse for a high-rise condo in Miami, something of home abides with them—and we are uncontrollably drawn to it.

Going Home

But what of people without a sense of home—physical or emotional? Can they find it along the way, or will they always be searching without ever feeling that warm blanket of comfort and acceptance? I pray this book has given those of you still wanting to find or create a real home of your own the hope that by following God's blueprint it can be done. I also hope that those of you who do have real homes have come to understand, as I have in writing about home, how blessed you are, and how imperative it is that you open your doors and hearts to welcome others into the homess you've been given.

The yearning to go home can be so strong that every other option pales in comparison. Not the yearning for home that we all have at the end of a long day or an exhausting trip, but the kind of yearning that resonates in the soul.

In my sixteen years of working full time, I saw many women who felt so pulled toward home my heart ached for them. Eventually, if career was too important to abandon, I would watch them alter their schedules in order to have more time at home with their children. If family finances permitted, they might just quit and go home, gladly ridding their lives, at least temporarily, of the classic struggle between career and family responsibilities.

I felt a yearning for home myself during the years my boys were young, but I also enjoyed my work and rationalized that as a single mom, I needed the income I was making, so I stayed where I was. That's why I was so surprised when I felt pulled even more strongly toward home after my boys were both grown and out of the house.

"Why, Lord?" I asked. "Why should I go home now when there's no one at home who needs me?" "Trust Me," was the answer I kept getting over and over. And so I gave notice and went home. Home to organize the closets. Home to find out what the cats do all day when there's no one around. Home to write all the things that had been on my heart for so long.

It's been an incredible experience. Although it was a scary decision for my husband and me to give up a steady income in exchange for the uncertainties of free-lance writing, the Lord has honored our decision by blessing my husband's business beyond our expectations. He's also provided plenty of rewarding work for me to do.

As a result, most days I feel that I have a balanced life at last. For me, the benefits include doing only the work I want to do, having time to visit our married kids and grandchildren, being in women's Bible study groups, volunteering, taking walks in the sunshine, and seeing hummingbirds at my window. For my husband, they include having a real baked potato for dinner instead of one popped in the microwave—and, he says, a helpmate for the daily demands of life.

Perhaps it's having the privilege to be at home more, even at this empty-nest stage of life, that has impressed on me the importance and the power of our homes. I know many women still can't afford to make the decision I made to give up a full-time salary for the vagaries of free-lance work. However, I've learned that even when we are away from home most of our waking hours, it's possible to have an attitude of simplicity, an attitude of abiding, that allows us to carry the peace of home with us wherever we go.

Furnishing the Homes We Build

When we think about building such a home, the most important advice we will ever get comes not from architects or developers, but from Psalm 127:1: "Unless the Lord builds the house, they labor in vain who build it" (NKJV). Our earthly homes won't be perfect, it's true, but we can rely on the Lord to help us make them the very best they can be.

May I suggest how to furnish such a home? Begin with a carpet of forgiveness. First, forgive your parents if they didn't create an ideal home for you to grow up in. Chances are they did the best they could with what they had. Forgive them.

Second, forgive yourself if (like me) you fell short of providing the perfect home for your children. After all, there is no such thing as a perfect home, remember? Chances are you did the best you could, too, and you need to forgive yourself and ask your children for their forgiveness.

Years after my single days were over and I was happily married again, I asked my two grown boys to go on a hike with me in the desert early one morning in May. We were in Tucson for my stepdaughter's college graduation, staying at a motel. They thought I was crazy to want to get up so early when we could all have slept in a lot longer, but they agreed to go.

My heart was heavy as we drove to the trailhead. I wanted to ask their forgiveness for my every failure as a mother—for divorcing their father and for serving leftover pizza too many nights in a row. The Lord had recently convicted me and forgiven me, freeing me from the guilt of my whole passel of past sins, but along with accepting His forgiveness, I knew I needed to ask my sons for theirs.

As we walked, I worked up the courage to explain why I had dragged them out of bed into the hot Arizona sun. I told them how liberated I felt because I knew my sins were forgiven, and how grateful I was for the truth of the Gospel that can set us all free from our failures. We talked a little, hugged a little, stared down a couple of lizards, and eventually they each told me I was forgiven.

As we drove back to the motel eager to jump into the pool and cool off, I asked if there was anything else I could do to make up for some of the pain they had to suffer as young boys and teenagers of divorced parents.

"Well, now that you mention it, Mom," my older son, Rob, said, "I think a ski boat would make me feel a whole lot better. What do you think, Tim?"

"Yeah. I think a boat would make me feel better, too," Tim replied. Nothing seals forgiveness like a good laugh. And no, they didn't get the boat.

Even with small mistakes, we must never hesitate to ask for our children's forgiveness. When we do so, we are showing them that they are also worthy of forgiveness. God sent His own Son to make it possible for everyone to experience newness of life. That's His blessing to us, and it's the source of all the power we need to pass a blessing from generation to generation.

So furnish the home you are building with blessings from wall to wall! The gift of the blessing is the way we tell our children that they are both loved and accepted, just as we are all loved and accepted by our Heavenly Father. If our children don't receive our blessing, they will have a difficult time passing a blessing on to their own children.

How do we pass our blessing to our kids? Family counselors John Trent and Gary Smalley have identified five critical steps to take. First of all, they write in *The Gift of the Blessing,* an effective blessing contains meaningful touch. Nothing beats a hug—but any loving touch will do. Second, the blessing must be in the form of a spoken message. We have to tell our children we love them over and over, not assume they know. Third, we need to attach high value to our children by letting them know how important they are to us. Fourth, we need to picture a special future for them, to let them know that we can see them accomplishing their dreams without putting great expectations on them. And fifth, we need to make an active commitment to fulfill the blessing by acting responsibly toward them.[2]

Letting Go

Part of passing the blessing to our children is letting them go, both emotionally and physically, when it's time. When we let go we are telling them we believe that they have the ability to go out and build homes of their own, and we are giving them the freedom to do it. They can't do so, and they can't ever joyfully come home again, even for a visit, unless we first let them go.

"You can't appreciate home till you've left it," O. Henry wrote. That being true, if we never let go of our children and allow them to leave home in every sense, they'll never be able to come back with an appreciation for all they left behind.

It isn't easy to let go, especially for moms. In my files I found a yellowed newspaper clipping that speaks to the whole letting-go process. It's a column by Ellen Goodman, of the Washington Post Writers Group, written when her only child, a daughter, was seventeen. She had instinctively reached out for her daughter's hand as the two of them were crossing the street. Both mother and daughter had laughed, but it was a poignant moment for the mom when she realized her role as protector was shifting.

When I read this column recently, my heart was tugged in a new direction. I realized that when I am with my mother now, I reach out for her hand to steady her as she walks. "I wish I could be there to hold your hand," she said to me on the phone last Christmas Day when I called her. "I always feel better when I can hold your hand." The mother-child relationship goes through many changes and shifts in roles through the years, all made easier by holding hands.

"I cannot fully chart the terrain of this mothering time," Goodman wrote in her column. "My sentiments will not fit on a card. But I do know that at the other end of the stage I am going through, most mothers hope they will have enabled rather than prevented this growing up. We want to be like the mothers we want to have: trusted resources in our children's lives. . . . We want to be the home they can come to, the base they can touch, the love they can count on, the place where they feel good about themselves."[3]

When I clipped that column, my older son was not quite sixteen. I hadn't gone through the letting-go stage, but my instincts told me that it was going to hurt, so I was gathering all the advice and comfort I could.

It does hurt to let go. But it's the hurt that comes from a necessary loss. It's something we have to do if we want to bless our adult children and the homes they are creating. Once we have let them go, they will feel free to return to our home without fear of losing their adulthood—and we will feel welcome in theirs. That's when we learn that we can have the feeling of being at home in many locations instead of just one! This is a reward we get for growing older and wiser. It's also a blessing we protect by keeping our opinions about houses, decorating, and childrearing to ourselves—unless they ask, of course!

I love visiting our married children in their homes. I wish they lived close enough for us to be able to drop by more often, but since only one family is within driving distance and the others are scattered from coast to coast, it seems we're always saving money and frequent flyer miles to go visit somebody.

Young marrieds move frequently, and we've visited a variety of apartments and rental houses—all authentic homes. A real joy, however, is seeing one of our young families finally settling in to a house of their own.

Last summer I flew back to New Jersey for my son Tim's ordination ceremony. He and Abigail and little Ellie, then seventeen months, had just moved into their first real family house, a "fixer-upper" in a nice neighborhood, so they hosted a big picnic in their new backyard. Discovering that the cooler full of pop was down on her level, Ellie decided to deliver ice to all the guests!

My mother flew in for the big event too. That sunny afternoon I watched with tears in my eyes as little Ellie toddled up to her great-grandmother to give her a piece of ice. Seeing her hand the ice to Nana I was reminded that every generation has a gift for those before and after it. And nothing makes a new house feel more like home than having four generations in the backyard at the same time.

"Having somewhere to go is home," reads another plaque on my kitchen wall. "Having someone to love is family. Having both is a blessing."

A Home Full of Love

A home furnished with forgiveness and blessing is probably also a home full of love. Family love is as close to unconditional, heavenly love as we can experience on earth. It's the kind of love we read about in 1 Corinthians 13: love that is patient, kind, and never fails. It's the love that is not easily angered and keeps no record of wrongs, but "always protects, always trusts, always hopes, always perseveres" (1 Cor.13:7).

Whenever I think of love that perseveres, I think about the love parents have for children who are in trouble or ill. Parents never give up—especially moms.

It could be a hormone that kicks in when a baby is first placed in our arms, or it could be a tenacity fueled by that unending supply of love. Wherever it comes from, the perseverance of mothers is legendary.

Moms of children with special needs seem to be given an extra dose of tenacity. A friend of mine with an autistic child has learned over the years to be her son's strongest advocate. Although she has accepted the reality of his limitations, she wants to challenge those limitations at every opportunity.

Linda's a small woman with dancing eyes and a generous smile, but when she senses something's wrong in Josh's world, she becomes a lioness on the prowl.

One autumn day, a surprise visit to his classroom confirmed her worst suspicions. While other children were working on computers, Josh was sitting in the corner separating bolts and screws. He found that extremely boring.

"He can learn and you will teach him," his mom declared to his teacher, and so it was. The computer gave Josh ways to express himself that he'd never had before, partially freeing him from the world in which he was trapped. Moms sometimes love ferociously—and they never give up.

A home furnished with love is also a home that knows love

can hurt. The young woman facing the break-up of a relationship or marriage knows love hurts. The parent whose child has taken a destructive path on the way to adulthood knows love hurts. The eighty year old watching a beloved spouse slip into the fog of Alzheimer's knows love hurts.

Children need to understand that love can hurt so they will learn to appreciate that love can also heal. A hug and a listening ear are signs of love's healing power at work at any age. Kids need to experience both often.

They also need to learn to recognize the many different faces of love. The outpouring of affection for cartoonist Charles Schulz when he died came in part from the simple messages of love he gave the world. Charlie Brown will return from the mailbox empty handed on Valentine's Day if that little girl with curly red hair rejects him again, but he will go home to a family that provides for him and a dog that accepts him just the way he is. He is loved.

The single woman whose friends call and want to get together is loved. So is the big sister whose little brother waits patiently by the door for her to get home from school so she can play with him.

We need to encourage our children to continue seeking and celebrating love in all forms, in spite of the pain it may bring, because of the incredible power it has to make life worth living. Nothing decorates a home like love.

Leo Buscaglia, in his jubilant book *Living, Loving & Learning,* writes, "I'm really convinced that if you were to define love, the only word big enough to engulf it all would be 'life.' Love is life in all of its aspects. And if you miss love, you miss life. Please don't."[4]

We must be purposeful about the homes we build, making conscious decisions about the role they will play in our lives in a physical and emotional sense. We need to commit ourselves to furnishing them with forgiveness, blessings, and love.

How do we do it? "But as for me and my household, we will serve the Lord," Joshua stated in Joshua 24:15. That's the focus and vision we still need for our homes today. We can't abdicate the responsibility God gave to each of us to create a home that honors Him. It takes such a home to raise children to be whole, productive individuals, and it takes many such homes to create the kind of village in which we all want to live.

Most of all, we must listen to the yearning in our hearts to simply "go home." Home to a place where we are forgiven and blessed. Home to a place where we are loved. Home to a place that doesn't have to be any certain place at all.

"This sense that you are really, truly home cannot be drawn up like a blueprint," wrote American writer Alice Hoffman. "It never depends on how many hollyhocks are planted beside the garden gate. It doesn't even matter if the front door leads to a three-bedroom ranch exactly like every other or a Victorian high up on a hill. . . . It's any house where the children sleep peacefully in their beds on winter nights, dreaming beneath warm quilts. It's any address where you realize—perhaps at long last—your own good fortune."[5]

A home is more than a place where people eat and sleep and leave their dirty clothes. A real home is where we feel loved, protected, and challenged to be all that God created us to be. This is the place in your heart I pray you have come to understand, to cherish, and perhaps to remember, as you turned the pages of this book. If so, welcome home.

Home Builders:

1. In what ways is home more a feeling than a place?
2. It may be too late for you to receive a blessing from your parents if they are gone, but it's never too soon or too late to give one to your children. Don't delay!
3. How have you furnished your home with love? How would an outsider recognize your home as a place where love resides?

Endnotes

......

Introduction
1 Charles R. Swindoll, *Home: Where Life Makes Up Its Mind*, (Portland, Oregon: Multnomah Press, 1980), 5.

Chapter One
1 Joni Eareckson Tada, *Heaven: Your Real Home*, (Grand Rapids, Michigan: Zondervan, 1995), 183.

2 Ibid., 16.

3 FamilyLife Marriage Conference, "A Weekend to Remember," (Little Rock, Arkansas: Campus Crusade for Christ, International, 1994), 18.

4 Mary Farrar, *Choices*, (Sisters, Oregon: Multnomah Books, 1994), 215.

5 Dennis Rainey, *One Home at a Time*, (Colorado Springs, Colorado: Focus on the Family Publishing, 1997), 50-51.

6 Anne Lamott, *Traveling Mercies*, (New York: Pantheon Books, 1999), 100.

Chapter Two

1 Brenda Hunter, Ph.D., *The Power of Mother Love,* (Colorado Springs, Colorado: WaterBrook Press, 1997), 224.
2 Lee Salk, *What Every Child Would Like His Parents to Know* (New York: Warner, 1973), 30-31.
3 Kathleen Parker, "New Child-care Study Results Are Flawed," *Orlando Sentinel, The Gazette,* March 8, 1999.
4 Christine Dubois, "Romancing the Mom," www.bconnex.net.
5 Nikhil Deogun, "Top PepsiCo Executive Picks Family Over Job," *Wall Street Journal,* September 24, 1997.
6 *365 Reflections on Mothers,* (Holbrook, Massachusetts: Adams Media Corporation, 1998), 105.
7 Hunter, 55.

Chapter Three

1 Frank Martin, *The Kid Friendly Dad,* (Downers Grove, Illinois: InterVarsity Press, 1994), 16.
2 T. D. Jakes, *The Lady, Her Lover, and Her Lord,* (New York: G.P. Putnam's Sons, 1998), 53.
3 Ibid., 133.
4 Kathleen Parker, "Having a Baby Requires a Dad and a Mom," *Orlando Sentinel, The Gazette,* March 26, 1998.
5 Janet Parshall, *Washington Watch,* March 17, 1999.
6 Karen S. Peterson, "Dads Missing in TV Action," *USA Today,* May 18, 1999.
7 *RealFamilyLife,* "Where Are the Fathers," July/August 1997, 8.
8 Ibid.
9 Ibid., 9.
10 William R. Mattox, Jr., "Promise Keepers Not About 'Women Haters,'" *USA Today,* October 6, 1997.
11 Ibid.
12 Suzanne Fields, "Evidence Is There—Dads Are Important," *Los Angeles Times Syndicate, The Gazette,* July 21, 1998.

13 Louise Silverstein and Carl Auerbach, "Deconstructing the Essential Father," *American Psychologist*, June 1999.

14 Charles Colson, *Breakpoint*, October 13, 1999.

Chapter Four

1 The Benton Foundation, "Kids Campaign," Washington, D.C., 1998.

2 Nancy P. McConnell, *I'm Home/Be Home Soon*, (Colorado Springs, Colorado: Current, Inc., 1984, 1988).

3 Jean L. Richardson, et al, "Relationship Between After School Care of Adolescents and Substance Use, Risk Taking, Depressed Mood, and Academic Achievement," *Pediatrics*, Vol. 84, 1989, 556-566.

4 Hillary Rodham Clinton, *It Takes a Village*, (New York: Simon & Schuster, 1996), 159.

5 Claire Cloninger, *A Place Called Simplicity*, (Eugene, Oregon: Harvest House Publishers, 1993), 87.

6 Ibid., 114.

7 Arlie Hochschild, *The Time Bind*, (New York: Henry Holt & Company, 1997).

Chapter Five

1 Dr. James Dobson, *The New Dare to Discipline*, (Wheaton, Illinois: Tyndale House Publishers, Inc., 1992), 51.

2 Ibid., 36.

3 Dr. Henry Cloud and Dr. John Townsend, *Boundaries*, (Grand Rapids, Michigan: Zondervan, 1992), 172.

4 Dobson, 6.

5 Barbara K. Mouser, *Five Aspects of Woman*, (Waxahachie, Texas: International Council for Gender Studies, 1995), 3.18.

6 Smart Shopper, 1-800-736-3055; "God's Rules" © Campbell for RTC.

7 Cloud and Townsend, 84.

8 Ibid., 90.

9 Ibid., 185

10 Douglas Belkin, "Mom's Candor Gives Other Parents Hope with Troubled Teens," Cox News Service Review, *The Gazette*, October 10, 1999.

Chapter Six

1 "Reggie White: Fighting the Good Fight," *Focus on the Family Magazine*, October 1999, 6.

2 Michael Ryan, "What Mom Knew," *Parade Magazine*, May 11, 1997, 6-7.

3 Kathleen Parker, "Children Need Unstructured Time to Discover Themselves and Others," *Orlando Sentinel*, *The Gazette*, date unknown.

4 Patti Martin, "Parents Don't Really Understand the Stress Children Face Today," Ashbury Park Press, *The Gazette*, March 13, 1999.

5 Barbara Mahany, "Parents Drive Free Time from Lives of Kids," *Chicago Tribune*, *The Gazette*, May 27, 1999.

6 Ibid.

7 William J. Bennett, *The Book of Virtues*, (New York: Simon & Schuster, 1993), 12.

8 "Preteens Say They Want More Talks with Parents," Scripps Howard News Service, *The Gazette*, March 1, 1999.

9 "This Week, Try Something New for Dinner: Good Conversation," (Washington, D.C.: Child Welfare League of America and The Honeybaked Ham Company, no date given).

10 Ibid.

11 Gene Edward Veith, "Don't Look Now," *World Magazine*, September 18, 1999, 16.

12 Mona Charen, "Television is a Seductive Monster," Creators Syndicate, *The Gazette*, August 26, 1997.

13 Ibid.

14 Robin Zenger Baker, "Turning Off the TV," *Welcome Home*, April 1996, 8.

15 M. Craig Barnes, *Hustling God*, (Grand Rapids, Michigan:

Zondervan Publishing House, 1999), 153.

[16] Thomas J. Stanley and William D. Danko, *The Millionaire Next Door,* (New York: Simon & Schuster, Inc., 1996), 3-4.

[17] Bennett, 14.

Chapter Seven

[1] Mary A. White, *Harsh Grief, Gentle Hope,* (Colorado Springs, Colorado: Navpress, 1995), 13-18.

[2] "Parents Don't Plan to Sue California Juice Company over Death of Daughter," Associated Press, date unknown.

[3] J. R. Miller, *The Home Beautiful,* (Grand Rapids, Michigan: Zondervan Publishing House, 1912), 172.

[4] Carla Williams, *As You Walk Along the Way,* (Camp Hill, Pennsylvania: Christian Publications/Horizon Books, 2001), publication pending.

[5] Ibid.

[6] Tim Smith and J. Otis Ledbetter, *Family Traditions,* (Colorado Springs, Colorado: Chariot Victor Publishing, 1998), 111.

[7] Neil T. Anderson and Steve Russo, *The Seduction of Our Children,* (Eugene, Oregon: Harvest House Publishers, 1991), 8-9.

[8] Miller, 77.

Chapter Eight

[1] Charles R. Swindoll, *Growing Wise in Family Life,* (Portland, Oregon: Multnomah Press, 1988), 36.

[2] Stephen R. Covey, *The 7 Habits of Highly Effective People,* (New York: Simon & Schuster, 1989), 138.

[3] Ibid.

[4] "In This Home," © 1997 Abbey Press, 1-800-962-4760. Used by permission.

[5] John MacArthur, *Successful Christian Parenting,* (Nashville, Tennessee: Word Publishing, 1998), 160.

[6] Linda Dillow and Lorraine Pintus, *Intimate Issues,* (Colorado Springs, Colorado: WaterBrook Press, 1999), 69.

7 Jane Johnson Struck, "Under Construction: An Interview with Jill Savage," *Today's Christian Woman*, January-February 1999, 70.

8 Bill McKeown, "Teens Lack the 'Assets' to Succeed, Survey Says," *The Gazette*, August 5, 1999.

9 For a copy of "40 Assets for Youth," contact the Search Institute, 1-800-888-7828 or www.search-institute.org.

10 Suzanne Fields, "Sobering Look at 'Tweens': 10-going-on-16," Los Angeles Times Syndicate, *The Gazette*, January 4, 1999.

11 James C. Dobson, Ph.D., *Home with a Heart*, (Wheaton, Illinois: Tyndale House Publishers, 1996), 182-183.

12 Dr. Henry Cloud and Dr. John Townsend, *Boundaries*, 132.

Chapter Nine

1 "Reaching the World on American Colleges and Universities," International Students Inc., 1999.

2 Elisa Morgan, "Momsense," MOPS International, November 3-4, 1999.

3 "Your Family, Our History," *Parade Magazine*, November 21, 1999, 6.

4 Charles Colson and Nancy Pearcey, *How Now Shall We Live?*, (Wheaton, Illinois: Tyndale House Publishers, Inc., 1999), 14.

5 Ibid., 15.

6 Philip Yancey, *The Jesus I Never Knew*, (Grand Rapids, Michigan: Zondervan Publishing House, 1995), 89.

7 Ina Hughes, *A Sense of Human*, (Knoxville, Tennessee: The Knoxville News-Sentinel Co., 1993), 4-5.

Chapter Ten

1 Lillian Schlissel, *Women's Diaries of the Westward Journey*, (New York: Schocken Books, 1982), 12.

2 Ibid., 55.

3 Cokie Roberts, *We Are Our Mothers' Daughters*, (New York: William Morrow and Company, Inc., 1998), 7.

4 Ibid., 8.

5 Barbara K. Mouser, *Five Aspects of Woman*, 3.21.

6 Ibid., 3.22.

Chapter Eleven

1 Charles M. Sell, *Family Ministry*, (Grand Rapids, Michigan: Zondervan Publishing House, 1995), 77.

2 Charles Colson and Nancy Pearcey, *How Now Shall We Live?*, 326.

3 "Catch the Spirit! A Student's Guide to Community Service," The Prudential Insurance Company of America in cooperation with The U.S. Department of Education, 1998, 2.

4 Charles W. Colson, "You Can Change the World," *Teachers in Focus Magazine*, May/June 1999, 23.

5 General Colin Powell (Ret.), "Pointing the Way for Youth," *SAM'S Club Source*, September 1999, 15.

6 "Home Schooling Up After Columbine Shooting," *EP News*, (date unknown).

7 Charles Colson, "God Governs the Affairs of Men," *Breakpoint*, February 26, 1998.

8 Robert J. Wicks, *After 50: Spiritually Embracing Your Own Wisdom Years*, (New York: Paulist Press, 1997), 16.

9 John MacArthur, *Successful Christian Parenting*, (Nashville, Tennessee: Word Publishing, 1998), 6-7.

10 Hillary Rodham Clinton, *It Takes A Village*, 96.

11 Charles M. Sell, 153.

12 Kathleen Parker, "This Mess Was Sponsored by the 'They' in the Mirror," *The Gazette*, November 2, 1998.

13 Beth Lueders, "Opportunity Knocks," *Discipleship Journal*, (Colorado Springs, Colorado: The Navigators/NavPress, September/October 1999), 63.

14 Charles W. Colson, "Clinton Care," *Breakpoint*, January 27, 1998.

15 Larry Crabb, *Connecting*, (Nashville, Tennessee: Word Publishing, 1997), 31

Chapter Twelve

1 Mary Farrar, *Choices*, 216.

2 Gary Smalley and John Trent, Ph.D., *The Gift of The Blessing,* (Nashville, Tennessee: Thomas Nelson Inc., 1993), 18-19.

3 Ellen Goodman, "Mothers Struggle to Let Go While Holding On," Washington Post Writers Group, *Rocky Mountain News,* May 10, 1986.

4 Leo Buscaglia, Ph.D., *Living, Loving & Learning,* (New York: Ballantine, 1982), 222.

5 Alice Hoffman, "It's a Wonderful House," *Architectural Digest,* December 1993. All rights reserved.